Out of
the
Darkness

SAMANTHA SIMON

SAMANTHA'S STORY

ARPress
ILLUMINATING IDEAS.
EMPOWERING VOICES

ARPress
45 Dan Road Suite 5
Canton MA 02021
Hotline: 1(888) 821-0229
Fax: 1(508) 545-7580

Ordering Information:
Quantity sales. Special discounts are available on quantity purchases by corporations, associations, and others. For details, contact the publisher at the address above.

Printed in the United States of America.

ISBN-13:   Paperback   979-8-89389-026-6
            eBook   979-8-89389-027-3

Library of Congress Control Number: 2024908744

Contents

Dedication

This book was written to help people all over the world; people who are depressed, in their darkest times of need. Please know that things will get better, please be strong. This book will demonstrate that after the storm, it always has to clear up and the sun always shines again. For every ying, there is a yang. The light will shine through, just believe and it will find you again. Be positive. Be patient. Your time will come. There is always good to all of the bad. It is what lights all of the fires within us and makes this world beautiful.

This book is dedicated to my mentors: my mother who was with me every step of the way, without her I don't know how I would have done it, I love you unconditionally. My grandmother, my angel and best friend who taught me the power of forgiveness and unconditional love and generosity.

To the absolute love of my life, my fiancé! Mark Naszradi, you are amazing. Without your love and support, I would be lost. You make me beautiful inside and out, I love you with my entire heart and soul. I am looking forward to spending forever with you. You are darling, my angel! I love you.

These pages will take you down a winding road of a true life story. It has many twists and turns, showing the power of belief and strength. The reason for me writing is to keep your flame lit. Never give up hope.

Chapter One

It was a brisk fall day in Marshall. Fallen leaves sprinkled the damp roads, lush lawns, and pointed roofs of the quiet town where we lived, draping all in a quilted blanket of reds, oranges, and yellows with just a hint of pale green. The distinct aroma of Michigan autumn permeated the atmosphere, blending the scent of freshly cut grass with the smoky musk of dry leaves and distant bonfires. I inhaled the bouquet, heeding its olfactory warning. I knew that I better enjoy the gentle fall chill and summer's last bit of lingering warmth, for Old Man Winter would soon be blowing into the Great Lakes region, preserving the town in a frosty time capsule during the long winter that lie ahead.

I relished the crisp air swirling around me, the scent of that familiar autumn potpourri infusing my smooth, strawberry blond locks as I unleashed every bit of might in my six-year-old body to propel my purple Schwinn Starlight at top speed. I was confident my bike was the best one around. It was my vehicle for escaping the world. The faster I rode, the better. I loved the way the wind would scramble through my hair, tangling it as only a furious breeze could do. I loved to pretend, and my imagination was at its most colorful when I was speeding on my bike. I would dream of my future and what it might entail. I would embody characters I knew from movies and TV, or I'd make up my own. The swiftness and intensity of flying on my bike only made the personifications of my imagination more vivid. Today, I was the Wicked Witch of the West in the *Wizard of Oz*. I rode faster, laughing to myself with my best evil witch cackle. The white stars that speckled my bike were blurry streaks to neighbors who were outside raking their lawns as I whizzed past. I rode high on the pedals, exhilarated, barely touching the banana seat as I lapped our cul-de-sac in record time.

Before I knew it, Dad was flagging me down in an effort to get me to stop riding and come inside for dinner. I skidded into the driveway at a sharp angle and reluctantly hopped off. The noisemakers on my spokes that were shaped as miniature soda cans made a tinkling noise as I walked and ditched the bike onto the front yard. I bounced up the driveway with the assuredness of a little girl who knows she's pretty darn cute. My face was a combination of my two parents. There was no mistaking me for anyone else's child. I had the almond-shaped eyes of my Japanese father and the nose, cheeks, and chin of my mother, who is one hundred percent Polish. A distinct mole sat in perfect placement over my upper lip. It stayed the same size as my face grew, so it's less prominent now, but at the time it was quite noticeable. To me, it was the ultimate beauty mark.

You see, it was 1987. Madonna had released her album *True Blue* the year before, and her movie, *Who's That Girl,* had just been released that summer. All things Madonna were 'in' with young girls at the time. We wore bangles, scrunched our hair, and based almost every fashion decision on what Madonna would do. Upper lip moles were a necessity, and I just so happened to be naturally blessed with the signature of America's biggest pop icon. I couldn't have asked for more. The other girls at school had to fake it by drawing one on their face with black eyeliner. Beyond the mole, I had smooth and flawless light olive skin. Lanky and tall for my age, I even towered over some of the boys in my class at school. Since my baby teeth had fallen out early, adult teeth grew in before my mouth could grow to accommodate them. This gave me an unusually large smile for someone my size. I was adorable, and I enjoyed being me.

I could entertain myself for hours. Aside from portraying characters while speeding on my bike, I loved the imaginary worlds of movies and television. My favorite cartoons were *The Smurfs*, *Gummy Bears*, and *Inspector Gadget*. I was obsessed with Barbie dolls and My Little Pony. Of course, *The Wizard of Oz* was my favorite movie. I still know every word of dialogue in it to this day. I watched it constantly, and naturally acquired a childhood obsession with Judy Garland. I was so taken with her performance, in fact, that I wanted to change my name to Dorothy. I would tell my friends, my family, and everyone

I met to call me 'Dorothy'. My request was often laughed off as silly and childish, but I was quite serious. I didn't like my name at the time, because there were three to five Samantha's in every classroom at school. My father finally told me that the reason he chose the name Samantha was because he found it to be the most beautiful of all the girls' names he had ever heard. That did it, and I started to forget about changing my name. From that point on, I thought of it as a nice gesture from my father. I still identified with Dorothy, though, much due to the recurring theme, 'There's no place like home', because I felt exactly the same way.

From my perspective, I had the ideal little family and a sublime life. First of all, I had two loving parents. Plus, I had two healthy younger brothers. We were spaced out perfectly—all three years apart. Since I was six at the time, Chris was three, and Cyle was almost one. It worked out nicely so that we all got our own quality time with my dad. Life was good for us. Some of my friends had a sick sibling, or they only had one parent at home, so I appreciated what I had.

I was happy and content, which gave me the security and strength to be independent. I would find a way to do what I wanted, no matter what. As a child, I spent an inordinate amount of time daydreaming about maturing from a little girl into a young woman. I contemplated how I would act as an adult, what kind of car I would drive, who I would marry. I had a Cinderella wedding all planned in my head by the time I turned twelve. One of my idols was Punky Brewster. I admired her creativity and thought she was super cool in general. One day, I went to school with two different shoes on, pulled my hair into pigtails, and wore a handkerchief wrapped around my right knee. The teacher called my mother at home and asked why she had let me go to school looking like that. Mom didn't know what I had done since I had secretly changed on the walk to school. I found the situation hilarious. I vividly recall other instances where I pretended that I was English like 'Mary' in *The Secret Garden*. I would imagine I was in the garden she could never reach, and I would run around exploring and admiring its beauty. Other times, I would turn an everyday playground set into a fortress sitting on a cliff surrounded by a stone wall. I would be the princess and the ruler of my kingdom, my backyard garden, and my horse and carriage sandbox chariot. I was a little girl who would always take long bike rides with my friends, run around in the front yard, have tea parties with my teddy bears, swing on the swings, and play make believe with my friends and stuffed animals. I also loved to read. To me, any book was a good book as long as it told a good story.

Though I had friends my age to play with, my best friend was my father. Half Japanese and half English, he considered himself to be an American mutt. He had thick, black hair that he wore neatly combed back with an inch of volume on top. He spoke through his actions and his eyes, which were deeply sincere. They were almond shaped and a dark, chestnut brown, indicative of his Japanese descent. His eyes gave away his feelings. When he smiled, he would squint, emanating an amused wisdom. When he was happy or pleased with something, I'd notice a twinkle in his eye. He was funny, sweet, and stern when necessary. He loved his children, and we meant everything to him. He was our hero and mentor. We wanted to be wise like him. He was not a man of many words, so when he voiced his opinion, we listened. He spoiled me with his love and affection, and I relished every single second of it. I looked up to him. I knew I could count on him for anything. With him, I felt content, happy, and complete.

I knew I was lucky to have such a wonderful father, but I didn't realize just how fortunate I was until I saw the way other parents treated their kids. Many fathers were not around much in the 1980s. Some of my friends' fathers worked constantly, acting more as providers than father figures. Others were absent and caught up in their own lives. Mine worked 8–4 so he could make it home by 16:30, just in time for our quality time. We had so many adventures together: going to the beach, the state park, fishing, or to the movies. We would dabble in hobbies or go to the toy store to reward good behavior. We would do anything that allowed us to appreciate and enjoy life. At the park, it was all about 'twirly' slide, which was my name for the slides that curved around and spiraled all the way to the ground. When we'd drive past a park that had one, I would ask my father to stop for me. He would every time. He was always doing whatever it took to make me happy. He was the father who would push me on the merry-go-round until I was nauseous, because he seemed to enjoy making me laugh and smile until I couldn't take it anymore. He fed off my happiness and laughter, and I adored him for that.

He was also a man of great wisdom and smarts where life was concerned. He taught me to be who I am today. He taught me to speak when necessary and to honor thy earth. He was fascinated with nature and had a deep respect for it. He endowed me with the golden rule, and I still abide by it today. I can almost hear him saying, "Just treat people the way you want to be treated". It was from my father that I learned to pause before speaking to think about what I was going to say and how I think the other person would feel should I decide to share. That simple life lesson has made me who I am. I credit my father's wisdom when people tell me I am very genuine and sweet. I treat others that way, simply because it's how I would like to be treated. Besides, I think life's too short to be angry or spiteful.

My father had a special appreciation for trees. To him, they were simple elements of nature that replenished his soul. Pine trees, oak trees, birch trees—if you can name a tree, my father loved it. Trees make it possible for us to breathe. My father felt we must give thanks to them, as we would not exist in their absence. "They are a part of our makeup and a part of the living whole," he would say. There was a certain poem my father would read to me, exhibiting that sincere squint of wisdom as he read it. I distinctly remember the last line, because I thought it was a little silly yet full of truth: "Poems are made by fools like me, but only God can plant a tree." When he read that poem, I could tell he thought the words were perfectly integrated to describe the importance of one of Mother Nature's most precious endowments—the gift of fresh air that allows us to live and breathe. My father loved planting trees. To him, it was a hobby and a labor of love. A natural landscaper and somewhat of a natural farmer at heart, he was very good at it.

Following Dad's lead, I, too, began to have a love affair with nature's gifts. I would spend the dark Michigan winters looking forward to springtime, when we would go to the nursery to plant our garden. My father didn't plant the standard rectangular garden like our friends and neighbors. He enjoyed being creative, working the garden into the design of the home and property, and complimenting the landscape. We had a typical backyard with a fence around the border. My father would dig up the soil around the outside of the fencing so that the garden outlined our yard. We placed starter tomato plants in the ground around the fence, along with seeds for green beans, pumpkins, cucumbers, red and green peppers, strawberries, and raspberries. We watered and waited, and watered and waited, and waited and watered. Weeks later, Mother Earth bore life to reward our hard work. Our little Midwestern fence garden was one of the most bountiful I've ever seen. It was incredibly rewarding that we had grown all of it by ourselves, and we could eat from the roots of our backyard. To me, it seemed like a miracle granted by God.

That spring, I had specifically picked out a seed pack for sunflowers. I liked them because they grew so tall and looked so happy. To me, sunflowers were the most important part of the garden. I adored the way they seemed so delighted to be given life. More so, they were taller than me, as they stood about four and a half feet tall. I was amazed that a flower could be as large as a small tree. Their magnitude enhanced their beauty even more, and I liked to think of them as supermodels with long legs. To me, sunflowers were appreciative, and I had a deep admiration for them. I liked to watch them sway with the wind, slightly bending as though they were bowing to us for the right we had given them, the right to life. They would lift up their leaf arms to the sun as it shone on them to give thanks and praise to the light for which we sometimes do not remember to be thankful. Every time I see a sunflower today, I get that same feeling of accomplishment, of tender and sweet contentment. I will cherish and cultivate that feeling within me for the rest of my life, for I find it incredible that something so simple can bring a person such rejuvenation.

Chapter Two

Throughout elementary school, I was what most called 'creative', 'funny', 'outgoing', and sometimes, 'a little bit out there'. I was definitely a dreamer with a vivid imagination. I shared the same playtime style as the *Muppet Babies*, which was an animated program with characters based on Jim Henson's *muppets*. Their toddler selves would play make believe when their Nanny left the nursery. They went on a new adventure in each episode. I enjoyed the idea of their imaginations taking them to places they had never been before, like pirate ships or beautiful islands, so I used its premise as a base for my own imaginary adventures.

As I grew, I maintained a strong personality with the willpower to do what I wanted. Clearly a child who possessed a deep urge to express herself creatively, I started to create story books almost as soon as I could hold a pen. I used my make believe journeys as premises for my own stories, inserting characters I'd created to propel the plots. I soon developed a strong adoration for writing, which I possess to this day. At the age of eight, I wrote a book entitled *Going to the Store*. It was a children's book about a little girl who took a simple trip to the store and turned it into an adventure. I hand wrote the story on lined paper, completing each page with little cute illustrations. My protagonist was colorfully descriptive about everything she liked and all she disliked about her outing. After returning home from the shore that evening, she told her father how much she loved him and how much she'd missed him that day. Looking back now, I know the girl I'd been writing about was me. For, although the story was fiction, it was similar to the way I thought of my family and my father.

Just as I am today, I was proud then of the fact that I had enough belief in myself and in the fact that dreams can come true that I wrote and illustrated an entire book. I even submitted my first handwritten and illustrated manuscript to a children's book publisher. I specifically liked the letter that I received back from the publisher. It had been typed on a typewriter and hand signed. It read as follows:

Date Here

Dear Samantha,

Insert letter…

Sincerely,

Publisher

I would like to thank **(insert publisher's name)** for keeping my flame of inspiration burning. Throughout the years, their words have given me the strength and inspiration to persevere and to continue to follow my dreams. I have always used that letter to give myself confidence in my motivation and belief to one day make it as an author. As I embark upon writing my story this time, I hold strong the knowledge that the lesson this book teaches will affect the change I wish to see in the world.

Back then, it was simply a hobby I enjoyed. I remember wishing I were an artist, instead, as I thought that coloring and painting required much more skill. In college, I had to write so much for my assignments that I began to think I no longer enjoyed writing. Now, however, I see writing as a skill. For me, it's a hobby that's non-negotiable. I'm thankful to have it as a creative outlet, and I see it as a required hobby. I've been told I have a gift for making something out of a thought, which makes me proud of my writing ability. The paper is my canvas, and the words are my creation. When I write, I like to imagine that I'm letting the words flow out onto the paper, as though they're the waves from the ocean crashing onto the land. In my opinion, one must be an avid reader in order to be a good writer. So, I've always read a lot as well. Reading also keeps the mind active and sparks the imagination. When you read a novel or a non-fiction, it can spark other ideas for books you may wish to write and helps you with the creative process. I've always enjoyed picking up tips from my favorite authors and incorporating them to enhance my own writing.

Chapter Three

The moment was ripe with power. My body buzzed with anticipation. I could feel the potential in every step leading to the entrance of the building. I'd been dreaming of this day for years. My dream was becoming a reality. I was sure everything was about to get exciting. After all, this was high school and anything could happen. I took in the grandeur of the building as I approached the door. The gigantic structure proudly standing before me dwarfed the cluster of rooms around a single hallway I'd called a middle school. I fully assumed every other kid I'd meet inside was grown up and super cool, which meant I was about to enter prime time as far as my life was concerned.

I lived too far from the high school to walk, so my mom drove me on my first day. This meant I could ask some of my friends to come along so I wouldn't have to walk those wide, congested high school halls all by myself. I would have protection and companionship of other friends who were just as nervous, afraid, and excited as I was. No way was I going to tell her I loved her and give her a kiss on the cheek when she let us out of the car. Someone might see me—like a senior, for instance—and think I was a baby. There was no way I would let something so controllable ruin my first day of school.

I was way too cool for that.

"Thanks, Mom!" I shouted as I slammed the car door.

There's no way to identify every emotion running through the mind of a young girl about to start high school: excitement, nervousness, and fear of the unknown are some of the most prominent. Excitement was the biggest for me. I had been looking forward to this day for as long as I could remember. In fact, I was so excited for my first day of high school that I made sure I wore the coolest outfit I owned. My days leading up to the start of school were spent putting together different combinations of my favorite pieces. I finally settled on an ensemble that featured a black and white vest reminiscent of 'Pebbles' from the *Flintstones*. Being that it was 1993, I paired it with tightly rolled jeans and a pair of black suede shoes with buckles. My hair was perfectly brushed and curled, which I topped off with the beau font poof that was rampant in the 1990s.

Gone were the days of that simple, tiny middle school. The monstrosity before me consisted of two floors, including a huge gymnasium, as well as a gigantic auditorium. The building alone was intimidating, even without the nerves of a thirteen-year-old about to enter into the youngest grade ever to be housed by this enormous structure. As an eighth grader, I was officially starting high school a year earlier than planned because in our hometown, the middle school had been torn down. Ten elementary schools would come together to be a single high school class of 1999.

With a deep breath, I mustered all the confidence I had in order to step inside. The hallways were vast and seemed to stretch for miles. I was instantly struck with the notion that it was possible to get lost within them like a rat in a maze. There was a rumor going around that if you didn't know where you were going in the building, the kids in the higher grades would play a joke on you and send you to the third floor. There was no third floor, so by the time you finished searching for it, you were late for class. I knew I didn't want to be late for class on the first day. Having kids snickering from across the room with all the attention concentrated on me would be mortifying.

I knew some of the kids from the other schools from the ice rink and my Little League softball team. Still, I thought of myself as a big fish in a little pond becoming a little fish in a huge ocean. I was eager to find out those typical things that are of utmost importance to a high school newbie. Who was in my class? Would I know anyone? With whom would I share a locker? Which lunch period did I have, and did any of my friends share it? Would I know anyone in my classes?

We had to bring our own locks for the lockers. Forgetting a lock meant you were taking a huge risk of someone stealing your locker. That was a definite no-no. You see, if you were booted out, you could end up with a locker by the seniors. Everyone knew you wanted to stay as far away from them as you could. I walked up to my locker, which was on the first floor level, and noticed a girl with long hair next to me. Her hair was so long and straight, it was down to the end of her back, almost to her waist. "Hi, my name is Jessica X. What's your name?" She looked at me like I was speaking some kind of foreign language.

"Uh, ha ha ha! Get a life, you dweeb," she said, scoffing at my vest. "This isn't a business forum." She laughed all the way down the hallway and around the corner. *So much for trying to make friends*, I thought. I figured that from there on out, I would just keep my mouth shut and mind my own business.

That's how high school started for me. I found out the hard way that there are just some cliques of people that aren't very nice. There are some people who get kicks out of making fun of people, being mean, and teasing. I knew that had been the case in middle school, but it was a different story in high school. In middle school, it was simple—there were nice people, and there were mean people. Considering myself to be a nice person, I simply stayed away from anyone who wasn't that way. Yet, once I got to high school, I soon realized there were multiple groups of different categories of people. It was no longer about being nice or being mean. Now, it was about being a specific way.

There were the jocks, the cool kids, the geeks, and the band geeks. The jocks, of course, were the athletic kids, anyone who played sports or who made it their business to be a sports groupie of any sort. They primarily got good grades and had a hard work ethic, as sports were about striving to be the best they could be. Naturally, they were very competitive, and to them, winning was everything. It wasn't win or lose—it was win or *nothing*. The cool kids were the pretty people in school. A lot of them appeared to be a bit catty and rude. Those gorgeous people in high school who care more about what they look like than how they treat people and since they were so worried about how they looked, they mostly treated people like shit because they were all about *them*. Next came the geeks, these kids were the super dorky kids who were strictly there to learn and then go home and do more homework so that they could be at the head of the class. And lastly, you had the band geeks. These were the kids who played in the high school marching band and were made fun of it for it. It was really sad because I was once really great at the saxophone but quit before high school because I didn't want to be labeled as a band geek.

I considered myself to be a little bit of three of the categories: geek, jock, and semi-cool, I guess. I wanted to be like those super cool girls but it seemed I didn't fit in with them. So, I kept my distance and left it at that. I was a geek because I truly had, and still have, a passion for learning. It intrigues me to learn new and interesting things and if I didn't get an 'A', I was upset with myself. My father had taught me how to get good grades and how important it was, so he would bribe me with a twenty dollar bill for every 'A' I received. It was a good strategy because it worked for me. I was a jock because I played sports and loved them. They were my passion in high school. I felt it to be very, very rewarding to win. It's an intangible thing but it makes you feel good to work so hard for something and watch it pay off.

I tried out for the basketball team in 8th grade because I was on the 7th grade basketball team and thought I could make it. Little did I know since I was short, only 5'5", I had a major disadvantage. There were girls on the team who were beasts and I couldn't stand the fact that stealing the ball from you was allowed. I liked to have control and felt very out of control in this sport. So, I then decided to try out for something different … the volleyball team. I had never even touched a volleyball. It always looked so fun, but they didn't offer it in elementary school. Bump set, spike! If you could remember and perfect those three elements, you were golden.

My father didn't agree with this, because he didn't think that eighth graders belonged in the same setting as high school seniors. I understand his point of view now, but back then I thought he was just giving me a hard time.

Chapter Four

The gurney jostled roughly as the paramedics snapped it into the securing device on the ambulance floor. I tried to brace myself as it tilted, but my arms were strapped down so tightly that I couldn't move them more than an inch. My eyes darted around nervously. Where were they taking me? A young female paramedic with short brown hair in a ponytail crawled in and took a seat on the bench beside me. I was surrounded by coiled cords, strange boxes with little blinking lights, and all kinds of mysterious machines and equipment. The compartment seemed to be filled with hundreds of secrets hiding places, a thought I found particularly frightening because I had no idea what I had done or why I was here. Who knew what they might pull out from any given nook or cranny or how they might use it on me? I started to panic. The ambulance had the sterile smell of untouched, freshly exposed metal and plastic. I caught a whiff of rubbing alcohol as she stuck a digital thermometer in my mouth.

"Try to hold still," said the paramedic, keeping a firm grip on my arm. Hearing the squeak of the back door as it began to close, I caught my last glimpse of the sky. The sun was setting. To me, it looked like what one might see on an African safari. The silhouettes of trees and buildings were alit from behind by the deep red, orange, and yellow horizon. That serene thought calmed me for a split second before the door slammed shut, locking me inside the tiny, intimidating cell. Unable to move with no idea of what was wrong or where I was going, my worst nightmare began. Something within me knew that there was no turning back from here. Paralyzed, I resigned myself to my new reality—constrained in the back of an ambulance with no idea where I was going, terrified and alone. I missed my grandmother now more than ever.

You see, my grandmother had been my best friend. For as far back as I can remember, not once did I see her without a cigarette in her hand, her mouth, an ashtray next to her, or two of the three. A lifetime of the habit brought on a case of COPD (Chronic Obstructive Pulmonary Disease), a progressively degenerative disease that's basically a combination of chronic bronchitis and emphysema. Once the battle ensues, there is almost no chance of recovery. The nature of the disease is that every day is worse than the last. It attacks a body and perseveres ruthlessly until there's nothing left of its victim. In the beginning, Grandma would complain that it took effort to breathe when she'd walk around the house. Before we knew it, she wasn't able to catch her breath, even when she was sitting down. The disease was attacking her lungs, deteriorating them until they eventually took on a sponge-like nature. Near the end, Grandma would pant and wheeze in her sleep through lips that were blue from lack of oxygen.

I was in the first semester of my final year of college when my grandmother passed. I was set to graduate the following spring with a Bachelor of Arts in Communications and a minor in Marketing. I'd made it my goal to someday become a pharmaceutical sales rep. The way I saw it, I could then one day help save people from deadly diseases like COPD. *To use this horrific experience for good might bring me catharsis*, I thought. Once she passed, I truly couldn't tell you whether it had been more difficult watching her suffer then or trying to go on without her. The reality of having spent the past seven years watching my grandmother gradually suffocate to death set in slowly. I had never experienced such a loss, and the resulting trauma infiltrated nearly every aspect of my life.

After about thirty minutes, I finally nervously asked, "Where are we going?" The ambulance driver did not reply. I tried again. "How long does it take to get there?" The paramedic in the back just looked at me and sighed. They weren't even treating me like a regular person. I was definitely in for it. I could feel it. The ride seemed like it would never end, but I wasn't so lucky. The ambulance slowed when it reached an aging, brick cube of a building. The hospital could easily have been mistaken for a prison, as it resembled a penitentiary more than it did a place to get well. A very tall, barbed-wire-topped fence loomed around the perimeter. The sheer appearance of it squashed any hopes of escape.

A piercing, desperate sobbing was audible as soon as the ambulance doors swung open. The sound got louder as I was wheeled down a dingy hallway. As we turned the final corner into a lobby, the source of the horrible sound came into sight. A slight woman sat redfaced, shaking uncontrollably. Her short, caramel curls bounced as she quivered. She was crying so hard that she began to lose her breath, coughing and sputtering, as tears and saliva expirated onto her clothing and the chairs and table close to her. Mature and well-coifed, she didn't look like the type of person who would throw such a childish tantrum. I'd never seen an adult act in such a way, and my bafflement distracted me for the time being before a young man's voice brought me back into the present.

"What are you doing here?" he asked. I turned to see a lanky young man in his twenties with sandy brown hair and a youthful face standing above me.

"What do you mean?" I asked in response. I didn't even know where 'here' was at that point. All I knew was that it was frightening and chaotic and that I'd rather be anywhere else.

"You don't seem to belong here," he rattled. "Are you signing yourself in? If I were you, boy, I would turn back now. There's no way you need to be in here. I take people here every day, and you're nowhere near as hysterical as they usually are."

I just stared at him, trying to figure out what he was trying to say, what this was all about. He wore the same white shirt with the same patches as the guy who'd driven me there. Since he was standing close to the sobbing woman, I figured he had to be her ambulance driver. I suddenly saw the image of my aunt's face, red and wet with tears as she hung up the phone earlier that day. I was far too upset to pay attention at the time, but now I remembered what she'd been saying to me.

"My aunt told me this was a place where people go when they're depressed, that I could get some help here. She said I need to be here," I spoke timidly, unsure.

"Suit yourself. It just doesn't look that way to me." With that, he walked out into the next lobby, letting the steel doors slam behind him.

Upon his departure, it seemed that the gravity of the situation hit me at once—the steel doors, the sobbing woman, the silent responses to my questions in the ambulance, the restraints. What in the world had I done? What was going to happen to me? I was terrified. Instinctively, I reached for my keys, but I had nothing. I had no purse, I had no car. I was locked in here. I couldn't leave. This was something out of a horror flick or a really bad nightmare, the kind where you can't wake up.

"Ms. Lowe?" An African American woman in dark green scrubs and a cream sweater stood in front of me. I hesitated out of mistrust, but soon realized that I didn't have much choice and decided cooperation was probably my best course of action at that point.

"Yes," I said.

"Come with me, please." She motioned to a door a few feet away. I proceeded to follow her into her office. It was a small area crammed with filing cabinets.

"I just need you to fill out some paperwork." She handed me a clipboard and a felt-tipped pen.

"What is this for?" I questioned suspiciously.

"This is for your insurance," she pointed to the top form before flipping to the next page. "These documents state what you brought in here, like clothing, your purse if you have one, and stuff like that. Don't worry; it's just the normal procedure." I appreciated even the slightest placation at that moment and took it as an invitation to get more answers.

"I have never been in a place like this before," I explained hesitantly. "I don't know what to expect … Do you know how long I'll be here?" She didn't miss a beat. I had the feeling she'd been asked the same question once or twice.

"Well, that depends on what your doctor thinks and whether you get better with time." *Weather?* What was she talking about? I was just tired! I tried to keep my composure.

"What do mean by 'get better'? I think there's been a mistake of some kind. I'm not sick." She looked at me with a gentle but firm expression that told me she didn't believe a word I was saying. I tried explaining, "I was just sad and exhausted, and I lost control for a little while. I don't need medicine or anything. All I need is some rest, and I know I'll be fine."

She wasn't entertaining my plea. I might have been tired, but I was still just as good at reading people as I'd ever been. I could tell she was becoming irritated with me.

"That is for you and your doctor to decide, Ms. Lowe. I am not a doctor. Now, let's get on with this paperwork. I have more people to sign in after you." I looked down at the clipboard as she pointed to different spaces at the bottom. "Sign here … and here … sign there." I was too tired and frightened to concentrate on reading what everything said, but all that autographing gave me the feeling I was signing my life away. Next, she took everything I had in my possession and made note of it on a piece of paper. "Remove the laces from your shoes," she said, motioning to my sneakers. That made my heart drop into my stomach. Was I a prisoner now?

"Why?!" I couldn't stop myself from the outburst. "What, you think, that I'm going to try to hang myself with them or something?"

"You never know what's going to happen here," she said with a matter-of-fact tone. "I have to do my job and make sure nothing like that occurs. Now, take the laces out, or you'll wear no shoes at all." Her voice had lost the calm, gentle tone it had had in the beginning, and her eyes were now wide and intense. I could tell she was angry and had no more patience with me. This was not a lady you want to mess around with, so I reluctantly pulled out the laces and handed them to her. She shoved the laces in a manila envelope without a word and sent me back to the lobby to await my floor assignment.

The hospital had three different floors. The top floor was for female inpatients only. The second floor was also designated for inpatients, but it was co-ed. The first floor was for the outpatients. Those were the lucky people who visited the hospital during the day, as students would their school. They got help but still got to go home at night and sleep in a regular bed like a normal person. *Good for them*, I thought sarcastically, having more than a sneaking suspicion that I'd be on one of the two upper floors.

Before the floor assignment, I had to get a wristband. This was so that the nurses could identify me should I drop dead. I was beginning to wonder why they rushed me to the hospital in such a hurry when all I was going to do was sit around and wait.

"Look what I got!" A slightly chunky woman with frizzy blonde hair and glasses shouted at me excitedly. I looked around. There was no one else she could be talking to.

"Are you talking to me?" She nodded frantically and reached into her bulky, red coat pocket. I fidgeted, distracted and uncomfortable. I didn't care what she had to show me, and I wished she'd just leave me alone.

"Flip it over." She held her pudgy palm out flat. A silver coin about the size of a quarter sat in it on display. Wanting to move along this exchange, I obliged and flipped it over. The other side of the coin had a hologram of an angel on it. I rolled my eyes and looked for a place to escape this woman, but it was too small a room, and there was nowhere I could go. She kept looking at me as if she wanted something. "So, it's an angel. Big deal," I said, dryly.

"Yes, I know," she said, her eyes growing more fiery by the second. "*You're* an angel." With that, she slowly walked back over to her seat and plopped down like a deflated balloon.

I felt as if I had just entered the twilight zone. What the heck was I doing here? I just wanted to go home. I had tickets for two to the *U2* concert for Friday (two days from now), and they had not been cheap. I wondered if they would let me leave for the concert and come back. Somehow, I doubted they would. This place gave me the distinct impression that this wasn't somewhere from which you could just leave and then come back later. Just then, I overheard a nurse telling a man at the reception desk that once someone has been checked in, the doctors have to decide for them when they can leave.

"It is just like a regular hospital," she said. Yikes. I had seen the movie *Girl, Interrupted* a few years earlier. If this place was anything like the hospital in that movie, I knew I was really in for it. After waiting for what seemed like about an hour and a half, a mousy nurse came for me. "You are going to be on the women's unit," she informed me. "Let's go." I winced as I followed her to the elevators, pondering whether I should refer to my new quarters as my 'room' or my 'cell'.

I was living the life of an animal with no rights. My every move was subject to another's power of control over me. In the past, I had never even wanted to take aspirin for a headache. Suddenly, I was being thrown into what the doctors and nurses called 'quiet rooms', where I was administered medication. They were shooting me up with Depacote against my own free will. It was an injection of a form of heroin, given to people who suffer panic attacks as a way to calm them down. When it takes you under, it's like you are being pulled into a deep, heavy sleep. There is no resisting it and no choice. It's not fun.

Upon being checked in to the hospital, I'd been told that this was a place where I could get better. Yet, somehow, I found myself growing thinner and thinner by the day. Where I once desired a more svelte body, I now hated my drab skin and bony hips and shoulders. The Depacote had nullified any enjoyment that I'd once derived from eating. Foods I used to relish tasted like very dry chicken that could not be forced down without difficulty. It was such a struggle to eat that I would only do so reluctantly, after much coaxing from the nurses.

The nurses and doctors who were supposed to help and look out for my best interests were only making me worse. While in the throes of a nervous breakdown, I had been first medicated and then diagnosed. With no evidence from an MRI, I was labeled a manic depressive and a paranoid schizophrenic. Though I had even started to believe it myself, my soul fought to be who I once was and always shall be—a strong and brilliant young woman. My face now streamed with tears as I hoped and prayed to one day become that person again.

Chapter Five

In and out of day group therapy, I had no patience. I wanted my life back. I so badly wanted to get myself back into school and finish my degree so that I could be a functioning, normal human being in society. I wanted to be off this medication that clouded my thinking and gave me strange side effects.

For one, I had never owned a pair of glasses and in fact, an ophthalmologist once told I that I had 20/20 perfect vision! With these drugs, I could not see at all close up, everything was blurry. It was very hard for me to read a book for I had to hold it far away just to see the words. It was so frustrating that I would just give up. Something I once loved and learned from, I was unable to do. It was eye opening, no pun intended. It made me appreciative all of those years I had perfect vision. I had taken it for granted. What about those people who were born blind? I cannot imagine what they go through, but they are strong and learn to cope without their eyesight. I admired them. They don't know what it's like to see. While another person who has perfect vision their entire life, realizes the little things we sometimes aren't thankful enough for!

Another strange side effect was my off-balance equilibrium, as I would go down the stairs. I would fear for my life, gripping the walls and handrails as I took each tiny step very hesitantly. Most people are so used to stairs they run up and down them and sometimes even jump down when they get to a low enough height. I was afraid for my life, every step I took, I felt like I was going to fall. It was so frightening that every step to the bottom was like an escape from falling into a black hole. I was that terrified. Sometimes, my uncle had to help me walk down the stairs and hold my hand like a baby. I couldn't do it alone.

These were all minor side effects compared to the effect the medication had on my mind. My mind was racing a mile a minute and I couldn't even keep up with things I would think of. I was always confused and had overwhelming paranoia. I thought people were after me and that I was constantly being watched. Imagine that, as if you were always being followed and didn't know why. So, I would make up these silly stories and reasons in my head.

One thought was that I was so smart that the President had people monitoring me to see exactly how much information I knew about the terrorists and about the things that go wrong in society. I thought that if I shared all of this brilliant information, his spies and agents would tell him and he would hire me to go and work for him. Again, my mind racing and thinking ridiculous thoughts, why is it that when people get on heavy-duty mind-altering medication, they think about the government? What triggers that thought and why is it so common? Unexplainable and never looked into, I guess. I would think that anyone dressed in black was part of the undercover spy operation to check on me in the hospital. I was always looking out for them and would make sure I never said anything that would get me in trouble or make me look bad. I thought up an illusion in my head but then played it up like it was a real, live process. I remember one specific instance: they had interns at the hospital that were shadowing the doctors. This one woman was dressed all in black and carried around a clipboard. I said out loud to her one day as she was walking by, "Hey, you can't fool me! I know where you are from." I was serious and stern about what I said.

"Oh, I am in intern and I go to Wayne State. I am job shadowing for a couple of months while I go to school for my psychology degree," she said in a nice way. She was pretty studious looking and maybe if I had been in a semi-normal state, I would have believed her.

"It's okay, I won't tell." I was referring to the fact that I really and truly thought she was a spy from the FBI. I thought the black was some kind of uniform. I also thought that anyone who worked for them had a spy device smaller than the size of a tiny speck in their ear that translated back to the government headquarters where they had big machines that could report back and compute what the people around them were saying.

I was thinking way too deep and obviously had a little too much time on my hands in there to be thinking of so much detail. There were days that were like that, where I would just think and think and think and think and think non-stop! It was a never-ending pattern. I was wondering if I would be like this forever. It was starting to become normal and it was part of the paranoia that was very hard to get past. I just wanted to be myself again. This wasn't me and it was like there was a little voice inside of me that said, *Help! I am still here. Don't give up on me.*

What I had figured out after I got out of the hospital was that the combination of the five kinds of medication I was on was what was making me think these crazy thoughts. I would have a racing mind day in and day out. I was a person who never used to like to take aspirin for a headache and here I was now taking medication for a paranoid schizophrenic. The mixture of the five medications didn't like me and who knows what could have happened had I been on them any longer than I already was.

I knew drugs were bad. I knew that street drugs were bad, but I didn't know the mixture of any type of medication has its downsides. Even if it is a drug approved by the FDA. Take Elvis, for example, he died of a drug overdose supposedly, well those were prescription drugs of the wrong mix and probably the wrong dosage. I am not claiming to be a doctor, but it doesn't take a rocket scientist to figure that one out. Any time someone mixes drugs with other drugs, street or prescription, it is mandatory that they should tell their doctor. There are certain kinds of medications that are forbidden to be mixed and can cause permanent damage and even death. And to think, they were handing out anti-depressants like they were candy. It was so pathetic.

These prescription drugs didn't seem to make me any better, in fact, they were making me worse as the days went on. My mom said the first time she came to see me and right after I had taken my first pill, I was drooling all over the place and couldn't even put my tongue back in my mouth, I was a royal mess! How can someone, not even a doctor, administer medication to a patient who hasn't even been diagnosed? Just because I was in a place where everyone is supposedly crazy, didn't mean I was permanently crazy. I wasn't there of my own free will, I was there because a family that I had trusted told me that I could find help here and get better. I wanted to get better and put all of this behind me … I was getting more and more drugged up to bandage the pain instead of letting it heal.

As I examined my own situation, I wondered how many other people in there had a similar situation. How many people in there were terminally or mentally ill, truly? Were there some that were just having a rough time in their life or were there people who had gone there to get help and by that time, it was too late, they were stuck addicted to these prescription drugs and labeled as a mentally ill person. I would never know and no one would ever tell me.

Then, these doctors ask you, "Do you have any cases of mental illness in your family?" So what if I do? Does that make me mentally ill automatically? I could argue that all day on nurture v. nature and we'd be going around and around in circles. The fact of the matter was, I wanted to get better and get back to myself in a state where I didn't need any medication to distract me from thinking what I thought, feeling emotions that I was supposed to be feeling and doing things that a person could do on their own any other day … read, sleep, drive a car, take a walk, the simple things in life. On these medications, I was stripped of those pleasures and couldn't even begin thinking about them without having tears well up in my eyes.

"What's the difference to you if someone is diagnosed with a mental illness in my family? Does that make my chances higher than the others here? Or am I off the radar?" I was one to get lippy with these doctors and they knew I was smart. "If I am so sick, let's see you take me down to a medical facility and get me an MRI. Measure my brain activity levels of serotonin and show me with real live proof that I am schizophrenic! Show me the proof. You standing there, looking at me like I am an alien creature does not convince me. I will make sure that my lawyers get in here and see what goes on, how you ignore us; you pretend and make us think you are helping us. You don't give a damn! And the moment I raise my voice to you, you shoot me up with Depacote and tell me how fucking insane I am! Is that the way you treat a human being who just lost her best friend and doesn't know how to handle it? Doesn't seem right to me, Ms. Doctor!" I was livid and screaming at the top of my lungs and I knew I was in for it once I shut up.

"That's quite enough, Samantha. I have heard it all and I am not putting up with your yelling. I will see you in a few days, maybe then you will have calmed down. And look at those jeans, why are they faded and almost ready to rip? You know we have washing machines and dryers here for you to do your clothes." With that, she walked, or hobbled, as I would have honestly described it, away.

I knew I wouldn't see her for 3–4 days and I was perfectly fine with that. I was sick of her bullshit. I was sick and tired of the cloudiness and the drugs. I was ready to ditch the drugs but according to the experts in the hospital, I needed them for the rest of my life. My aunt told me I would have to be on them forever and there was no turning back.

The drugs I was on were the following, I still have the paperwork till this day and I don't know if there was a combination of all of these at the same time or not because they were constantly increasing or decreasing the dosage and changing the medications. I remember, one time, they even gave me a drug that was meant to stop people from having seizures to offset all the horrific side effects these pills gave me, how odd was that? It was like, here take pills #1, #2 and #3 and take #4 should you have side effects and even if you don't, you won't know any way because you'll be so numb to the world you won't know what's going on. That's how I felt.

One drug was called Oxcarbazepine (ox-kar-BAY-zih-peen) and according to the prescription, it is a generic drug to the drug Trileptal. Under the heading uses, it states, 'This medication is used to treat seizure disorders (epilepsy). It may be used with other seizure medications as determined by your doctor.' How to use: 'Take this medication by mouth, usually twice daily. This drug may be taken with or without food. Do not stop taking this drug suddenly without your doctor's approval since seizures may reoccur.' Side effects: 'Dizziness, drowsiness, general weakness, nausea, vomiting, rash, headache, dry mouth, or constipation may occur. If these effects persist or worsen, notify your doctor. Tell your doctor immediately if you develop any of these serious side effects: vision problems, loss of coordination, trouble walking (abnormal gait), uncontrolled muscle movements (tremor), and stomach pain. Tell your doctor immediately if you develop any of these unlikely but serious side effects: trouble breathing, mental/mood changes, persistent sore throat or fever. Tell your doctor immediately if you develop any of these highly unlikely but very serious side effects: chest pain, unusually fast or slow heartbeat, one-sided weakness or slurred speech, bloody diarrhea or coffee-ground vomit.' Yum.

Out of the lengthy list of side effects, I was experiencing the following: dizziness, drowsiness, dry mouth, constipation, vision problems, loss of coordination, trouble walking (downstairs only for me), and mood changes. Okay, then I was in the odds of major side effects from this one.

The other drug was called Clonazepam (klo-NAY-zeh-pam) and according to the prescription pamphlet, its common brand name is Klonopin. Uses: 'This medication is used to treat seizure disorders or panic attacks.' How to use: 'Take this medication exactly as prescribed. Try to take at the same time each day so you get in the habit of taking it. This medication may be taken with or without meals. However, if upset stomach occurs, take with food. Use this medication exactly as directed by your doctor. Do not increase your dose, use it more frequently, or use it for a longer period of time than prescribed because this drug can be habit forming. (Wonderful!) Also, if used for an extended period, do not suddenly stop using this drug without your doctor's approval. Over time, this drug may not work as well. (So, it's a short time drug, it could make me addicted to it, but first, I have to find out if my human, error-prone doctor gives her blessing, are you freaking kidding me!)? Consult your doctor if this medication stops working well.'

Side effects: 'Indigestion, change in appetite, nausea, seizures (hmm … that could have triggered the panic attacks), drowsiness, dizziness, headaches, tiredness or weakness may occur. Mood changes, sleeplessness, excessive hair growth or loss of hair (what the heck), blurred vision, dry mouth, sore gums, change in sex drive, muscle pain and weight changes may occur. If any of these side effects persist or worsen, inform your doctor (lovely, so they can drug me up some more?). Notify your doctor if you develop double vision, unusual eye movements, severe weakness, increased salivation, hallucinations, loss of coordination, a rapid or pounding heartbeat, difficulty speaking. In the unlikely event you have an allergic reaction to this drug, seek medical attention. Symptoms of allergic reaction include: rash, itching swelling, dizziness, trouble breathing. If you notice other side effects not listed contact your doctor or pharmacist.'

Of those listed side effects, I experienced the following: change in appetite (I couldn't eat) drowsiness, dizziness, tiredness, weakness, mood changes (like you wouldn't believe: happy, sad, then tired and then happy, excited and on and on), blurred vision, weight changes (I looked anorexic), hallucinations, loss of coordination and difficulty speaking.'

Phew, that's scary! Then it says on the pamphlet: 'tell your doctor of all drug interactions especially certain antidepressants and anti-seizure medication.' Well, the last one I described, Oxcarbazepine is an anti-seizure medication. Hmmm.

The next drug I was taking is called Benztropine. I remember the doctors calling it Cogentin, this must have been the generic name, Congentin is the brand name. Uses: 'This drug is used to treat symptoms of Parkinson's disease or involuntary movements due to the side effects of certain psychiatric drugs.'

Oh great, so this drug was given to me to offset all of the side effects of all the other shit they were giving me? What was I, their freaking lab rat? I am a human being with a brain that is fragile, are they fucking crazy? Those doctors don't even know how the chemical reactions work with one another, what the fuck were they thinking? I asked for an MRI for hard, physical proof that there was really and truly something wrong with me. They ignored my demands. I put in the box that was supposed to go the state to get my rights; they once again, ignored my wishes. This had turned into a money thing. They were milking my insurance for all it was worth, sucked it bone dry and then let me go to the wolves. Nice diagnosis, doc, a paranoid schizophrenic. Since when does a normal functioning human in society turn like that after a death and have that title tagged on her without even physical proof. Unbelievable. The more and more I think about it; the more the hospital and doctors screwed me. They were so wrong to not be more careful with me. But hey, they're human right, they can err.

Okay, back to the Benztropine pamphlet. How to use: 'Take with food or milk to prevent upset stomach, unless your doctor directs you otherwise. Take this drug as directed. It may take a few weeks or months before the full benefits of this medication are observed. Do not stop taking this medication without your doctor's approval. Suddenly stopping the medication can sometimes lead to worsening symptoms.'

Side effects: 'This drug may cause drowsiness, dizziness, headache, loss of appetite, stomach upset, vision changes, sleeplessness, trembling of hands or dry mouth. These effects should subside as your body adjusts to the medicine. If they persist or worsen, inform your doctor promptly. Notify your doctor promptly if you develop: vomiting, chest pain, difficulty swallowing, difficulty urinating, uncontrollable movements, rapid heart rate, skin rash, mood/mental changes. To relieve dry mouth, suck on (sugarless) hard candy or ice chips, chew (sugarless) gum, drink water or use saliva substitute. If you notice other side effects not listed above, contact your doctor or pharmacist.'

I had experienced the following side effects: drowsiness, dizziness, loss of appetite, vision changes, sleeplessness and dry mouth.

This one was not as bad as the others. Why would they give me a drug to subside the side effects? This was a little or a whole lot over the complete top! I was forcibly being put on all of these medications. I told them I didn't like to even take aspirin and they ignored me. Who the fuck did they think they were? Had I been in the right mind, I would have walked the hell out and never looked back. Laughed in their face and told them to pound sand. That's an expression that means go do something worthless. The more I look into this, the angrier I get, how could they do this to me? I never tried to kill anyone or kill myself. I had a really bad reaction to a medication and then was told some wrong advice and was in the wrong place at the wrong time.

The last drug pamphlet on the attached prescriptions is called Risperidone (riss-PAIR-ih-doan). The common brand name is Risperdal. Uses: 'This medication is used in the treatment of psychotic or mental conditions'.

Side effects: 'Dizziness, drowsiness, nausea, increased dreaming, nervousness, loss of appetite, dry mouth or fatigue may occur the first several days as your body adjusts to the medication. Weight gain, vision changes, decreased sexual desire and insomnia have also been reported. If any of these effects continue or become bothersome, inform your doctor. Notify your doctor if you develop: rapid/pounding/irregular heartbeat, skin rash, itching, difficulty moving, muscle stiffness, muscle spasms or twitching, sweating, involuntary movements (especially about the face or tongue), drooling, tremors, trouble swallowing, mental confusion, seizures. Tell your doctor immediately if any of these unlikely but very serious side effects occur: one-sided weakness, numbness in the face arms, legs, vision problems, slurred speech, confusion. Males—in the unlikely event you have a painful prolonged erection, stop using the drug and seek immediate attention or permanent problems could occur. If you notice other side effects not listed above, contact your doctor or pharmacist.'

Okay, whew! So glad I wasn't a man taking that one, could you imagine that? Doesn't sound like something that can make you better, it sounds to me like it can make you worse in the likelihood you experience the symptoms. Of those symptoms, I had the following: drooling, mental confusion, seizures (I had two major ones, more like panic attacks), loss of appetite, vision changes and confusion.

As you can see, these drugs are very bad for you if taken in a large dose that may not be appropriate for your body weight, the interactions are dangerous and the side effects definitely outweigh the positives. What are the positives? For me, they were nothing. All of these drugs lied, they didn't help me one single bit. They made me worse. I have never felt so bad in my entire life! I was a zombie, I was paranoid, I believed anything anyone told me, (which could have been very dangerous!), I was scared, I was ready to get myself back.

The doctors kept saying over and over again, just wait; give the meds time to sink in. Your body has to adjust. And then when a drug was too overpowering for me, they would give me another one to replace, and there goes the vicious cycle. It was a never-ending battle; it was the worst thing I ever experienced. I wouldn't wish any of these symptoms and side effects on my worst enemy.

Drugs may be the answer to some people; they just weren't the answer for me and definitely not in that dosage and interaction. I was a complete mess. There were more side effects of which I will get into later in the book; there were strange experiences and strange people with mental problems surrounding me. The more and more I saw people get hooked on these meds, the worse I began to see the effects. The hospital was a gold mine. It was a gold mine to milk insurance companies and then poof, insurance runs out, you're all done. Bye-bye, just like that. My mother's attorney predicted my release, she said just wait, be patient, let the insurance run out and she will be set free. That's how it happened. Drugs just weren't the answer for me.

Chapter Six

Ring … ring … Each ring seemed to be lasting four times as long as usual. Would anyone ever pick up the phone? Finally, a voice answered. I gave him no chance to speak.

"Hello, is this the radio station? Yes, I believe that all children are created equal. And, if you pass the sign on I-94, it says 'Persistence Pass' on it with a picture of Abraham Lincoln. Have you ever seen it? It is a great sign, and it is the truth, you know. Hello, hello? Are you there?" He had hung up on me. I was in a manic, hyperactive state.

That hysteria was a side effect of the antidepressant I'd been prescribed by my doctor that was supposed to make me better. After the loss of my grandmother, I had mentioned to my doctor that I was depressed. I remember him saying that people who are depressed and sad can, "Kill themselves in their heads". He said that when this happens, their brains essentially begin to eat themselves, and they deteriorate.

"Take these," he said, "one per day," and handed me a mysterious prescription. I'd never heard of the medication.

That was the beginning of the end for me. Instead of preventing my own mental self-sabotage, the medicine had the reverse effect. I went absolutely nuts. The drug made it impossible for me to live my life normally. I couldn't drive or even perform the simplest of tasks.

My behavior and my emotional state were completely unpredictable. I was a different person from moment to moment. This rendered school nearly impossible and made it extremely difficult for me to hold down a job.

The radio station incident occurred on my third day of taking the medication. That medication took immediate hold of my mind and brought me on one crazed, rollercoaster of an adventure. It was like my mind was moving at the speed of light, bouncing all over the place, and I was frantically trying to keep up with it. I wasn't able to sleep, think straight, or eat. At the time I made that call, I'd been up for three days straight, during which my entire nutritional intake had consisted of half a cheeseburger and a half glass of milk. I spent time just staring at the TV Guide Channel in an attempt to make logical sense out of what the numbers meant and how the titles of movies and programs on television were related. I even found myself speaking out loud in a way that reminded me of something out of a scene from the movie *A Beautiful Mind.*

I was on my own, then, living with a roommate like a normal x-year old. My roommate overheard my hysterical call to the radio station. Concerned, she called my mom. Of course, my mom was afraid I would do something crazy or dangerous, so she told my roommate to call the police. She wasn't trying to be mean to me; she was acting out of concern for my well-being. While we waited for the police, I went to my room to access the stash of tip money I'd saved from a waitressing job I'd had. I grabbed some of the money and tore it up in my roommate's face.

"You see this? This money here? It means nothing. No one cares about it, and it can't save you! It can't save me, and I just ripped it up. That is how much I care about it! I ripped up a hundred dollars!" I probably would have ripped up more, had I had more. Thank God I didn't. My roommate couldn't do anything but stare in empathetic astonishment.

By the time the police got there, the place was a wreck. I had completely trashed my room. To make matters worse, I looked heinous. I had on flannel pajama pants with an unmatched oversized t-shirt and a cream-colored robe with leopard fur on the collar. I had dyed my hair black (far too harsh and ashy of a color for my olive skin), and it was slick with grease. I was pale, too skinny, and practically hyperventilating. I could hear my rapid heartbeat getting louder and louder … *thump, thump, thump*!

"Are you okay, ma'am?" a rosy-faced police officer asked as he approached me.

"I am Superman. I can fly and save the world. I want to show you how I can jump off the roof and fly far, far away! I want to save the children from cancer and tell them everything will be okay. I want to be like Princess Diana and do great things for the world! You know 9/11? Well today is 12/11, and the terrorists are still on the loose! We have to save ourselves from them. Protect the children! Protect the children! The schools are being bombed! My brother's school is going to be bombed!"

On and on I went, rattling nonsense. I talked about how the cure for everything was ice and water, and how the only way to make yourself better if you are sick is to drink a lot of water until you can't take it anymore. I was having a bad reaction to the antidepressant. I was incredibly agitated and excited, and I desperately needed to come down.

"Ma'am, the ambulance is here. Everything is okay, but you have to come with us. They are going to take very, very good care of you. Don't worry," the police officer assured me.

They escorted me outside where I could see my mother from the corner of my eye. She was with a friend, but I was too incoherent to recognize who it was. My mother was hysterically crying and could barely speak or even breathe. Her mascara was running down her beautiful olive skin as though she had cried through the entire drive to my place. Her eyes were wrought with pain and intense sadness. As deluded as my perception had been by that drug, I could tell that this was the most dreadful, shocking sight my mother had ever witnessed.

"Ma'am, what have you been taking? Are you on drugs?" the police officer grilled me as he walked me to the ambulance.

"The only drug I took was my antidepressant, that's it. I have not taken anything illegal!" I was on a major high from the drug, so everything I said was overemphasized, as though I was too excited for words. I was shouting every sentence at the top of my lungs.

"Are you sure ma'am, is that all?"

"Yes! I'm *sure*! I am so *sure*!"

"Well, ma'am, we still have to search your car and bedroom." He spoke with authority. "You know that if we find anything, we are going to have to tell the doctors. Don't worry, though. It's just for your safety. Okay?" He had sincere eyes, and I stared into them for a brief moment. His eyes were huge and a deeper blue than I had ever seen. I saw the sky when I looked into his eyes, as if they went on forever. Though his head was closely shaved, like a military cut, I could tell that his hair was sandy blonde in color. Those eyes and that hair seemed intensely familiar.

"You look like my friend, Annie's, dad. Are you her father? She never met her father, and he doesn't even know she exists! Are you her dad? Really, come on. Tell me the honest to God truth. Are you? Are you!?" I was still screaming, and by now, I was having trouble even catching my breath.

"No, I am not her father," he said simply. "Get well, ma'am, okay?" He then passed me on to the care of the ambulance driver.

"Miss Jenn, hello there. Come on in," the paramedic said. I complied, but not before I screamed as loud as I could, "*Princess Diana!*"

"Is this for me? Do I get to ride in the ambulance? Wow! I am so excited. I have never ridden in an ambulance before. Are we going to get to put the siren on and everything?" I asked. I was now beginning to sound like a small child, while panting like an agitated animal.

"Why, yes, you are going to ride in here. We are just taking a short trip. We may use the sirens if needed, but we normally only do that for emergencies." He was a happy man, and I sensed he had a strong femininity to him.

"I need water. I need water!" I kept saying it over and over again. "Can I drink this water?" I said as I reached for what appeared to be some kind of liquid for IVs.

"Nope, can't drink that water. It is not for that."

"What is it for then?" I said curiously, reaching for it as if it were a soda.

"It's irrigation water, and it is poisonous," he said in a stern manner. I began to understand that he really didn't want me to drink the water and decided to give up on asking. I was staring out the back window and noticed the cars tailing the ambulance. I instantly recognized the driver of the car behind us as the President himself. To my delight, his daughter was with him. I was now hallucinating.

"Do you see them? Do you see them?! Oh, my God!" I was screaming at the very top of my lungs. "It's George Bush and his daughter! They are waving at me and smiling! Hi, George!" I was seeing people who weren't there. I was thinking crazy thoughts. I had become what I never believed I could be.

I rambled on and on for the rest of the ride. I was talking nonsense and talking just to talk. The paramedic was very kind and answered every question I threw at him. Finally, I decided to ask what I had been wondering all along. "Can I ask you a question without you thinking that I'm trying to be mean to you?" I asked hesitantly.

"Sure ... ask away." He spoke kindly.

"Are you gay? I can just tell. You seem like a nice person, and I am not trying to offend you. I just wanted to make sure what I was thinking was right."

"Yes, I am. I am gay," he said with assertiveness. I felt as if he'd had to answer that question before and was used to the fact that people were curious about that.

"Well, good! I love gay people! You are all so nice and friendly. As a matter of fact, I am glad you are gay."

"Why, thank you. I've actually never witnessed that type of reaction." He began to smile. He was such a nice man, and even though I was submerged in the wrathful effects of the antidepressants, I could tell he felt sorry for me. I would see sadness cross his face when he heard me say things that didn't make sense.

"Are we there yet!?" I exclaimed like a little girl on her way to Disneyworld. I wanted to be there so I could show them that I was not under the influence of recreational drugs. I felt that I had to convince everyone that this was a drug that was prescribed to me. I wanted to prove it to the doctors, to everyone.

We parked right in front of the hospital. I hopped out of the ambulance and began to skip to the entrance. I felt like I was in the *Wizard of Oz*, happily traveling down the yellow brick road. The only part about this Oz was that there weren't munchkins or fairy godmothers. There weren't lollipop leagues or ruby slippers. There were very sick people. There were doctors inside telling people that their family member was about to die. There were people finding out that their loved one had just been diagnosed with cancer. There were individuals who were sick in the head and needed psychiatric help. This time, I was one of those people; not by choice, but by accident. I needed help. I needed to come back to reality and know that everything was actually all right. I needed to know that it was possible for me to return to the life I had and that all I needed to do was to help myself. What I didn't know then was that my condition was serious, and I had a long road ahead of me.

At the hospital, they pumped my stomach to expel any remaining part of the drug that might be in me. I was honest with them and told them that I had only taken what the doctor prescribed to me, one pill each day. The nurses at the hospital didn't believe me. They thought I had taken other drugs in addition to the prescribed Lexapro because of the way I was acting and the fact that my pupils were dilated.

When they pump your stomach, they make you drink charcoal, which induces vomiting. I was not cooperative. I didn't want what they were giving me, and I didn't want to vomit. I could have vomited but I was too stubborn. If you ingest the charcoal and you can't vomit, you then defecate instead. Charcoal isn't friendly when it's coming out that way. It's excruciatingly painful.

"She's right," a nurse said when she returned with the results. "The only form of medication we found in her system was the Lexapro. It obviously did not cooperate with her system to make her react this badly."

The doctor looked at me and said, "Hello, Samantha, my name is Dimitri."

"You have a nice name, Dimitri," I said with a raspy voice.

"Samantha, why did your doctor tell you he was prescribing this medication? Were you depressed?"

"Yes, I was upset that my grandmother had died, and I felt depressed. So, I went to my gynecologist. He told me that I would only get worse if I didn't get any help." I was getting sleepy at that point, and it was evident in my voice.

"Samantha, I know you think that the doctor was trying to help you. However, the fact is that he had no reason to prescribe you this medication. He is not that kind of doctor. You could have been seriously hurt, or you could've harmed someone else. Your body's response to the medication was similar to an allergic reaction. We are going to have to keep you here overnight for observation. I will come by to make sure you are okay. For now, the nurse will handle your belongings and make sure that you get something to eat. How does that sound?" He was a pleasant man with an accent, though I wasn't able to decipher its origin.

"I'd rather go home, but okay." Given the events of the day, I decided at that point it was in my best interest for the doctors to decide what was best for me that night. "I'll stay," I whispered sleepily.

My mom had gone home. When she returned, she told me that the doctor said I just needed rest and relaxation. I had a lot going on and I was exhausted. I wasn't allowed to work, to go to school, or to do anything else that might place me under any strain until two full weeks were over. My mom hugged me goodbye and said she would see me in the morning.

They placed me on the fifth floor, which was dedicated primarily to oncology. It was eerily quiet. I was placed on 24-hour watch for protection. They wanted to keep a close eye on me to make sure I didn't do anything crazy or harmful to myself. I thought they were doing this because they wanted to babysit me.

The watch people would work in four-hour shifts, quietly walking the dimly lit hospital hall. Some were nice and friendly; others were professional and kept to themselves. Each person had a different personality. I liked all of them, though. The doctor and nurse would check on me every now and then. In this hospital, they didn't give me any medication. They just observed me like a science project Petri dish, as if they were waiting for bacteria to grow.

I awoke the next morning inspired by a brilliant idea. I would call my entire family: aunts, uncles, everyone. I wanted to tell them all where I was and invite them to come and visit me. Now that I look back on it, I think I just wanted sympathy.

My mother had two stepsisters, Kathy and Patty, who seemed to be attached at the hip. I didn't think they ever did anything without each other. I found it cute, and it made me want a sister. Kathy's husband, my uncle Stu, just so happened to be in the very same hospital for heart surgery. My mother and Kathy never got along, and I'd always hoped for them to reconcile. While I truly liked Kathy, I understood that she had a sort of *Jekyll and Hyde* personality. One minute she would love you, and the next, she couldn't even look at you. A bona fide control freak, she was always striving for perfection. She was the baby of the family, always picked on by her siblings as a child and clearly favored by both my grandparents. Perhaps this was why she always thought that her way was the right way and why she was always trying to control everything and everyone. I saw her in action when my grandmother was alive, always trying to control my grandmother's affairs. She even went so far as to have my grandmother prescribed Prozac against the wishes of the rest of the family.

Kathy and Patty tiptoed timidly into my hospital room, as if they were trying not to wake a sleeping baby. Clearly unsure of what was happening, they were very much taken by surprise to see me lying in a hospital bed.

"What happened, Samantha?"

I told her the whole story—that I had been depressed about my grandmother passing away, that I'd gone for help, and that the medication just didn't agree with me. This was simply a result of my body rejecting the medication. I told her that even though I'd seen it as a punishment at the time, I now knew that it had helped me on my path and that this experience would help save others.

As I told my story, I watched Kathy's face shift from worry and concern to fear, even terror. Her eyes were big and bulgy as she looked at me, as if they were going to pop out of her head. Though I liked her, I had never been sure whether she really cared about me or not. That day, though, Kathy listened to me with compassionate ears. At that moment, I felt that she did love me, and I knew she was there to help. In all the craziness, I felt an immense love. Kathy was there for me. I knew I was safe when she was talking to me. Plus, she had the means to properly care for me because she was a nurse practitioner. She even traveled around the world, speaking to doctors about medical issues. I knew she was paid a lot to do so. I trusted her completely when she gave me any medical advice regarding medication. In my eyes, she was the expert. For the first time in a long time, I felt content.

Chapter Seven

"Time to check your vitals." Despite the fact that it was pitch black and I was sound asleep, the nurse spoke at a normal volume, jarring me awake.

"What time is it?" I asked sleepily.

"5:30 a.m."

I groaned. I'd never been a morning person, nor did I care what my freaking heart rate was at the crack of dawn. She took my temperature, blood pressure, and pulse. "You're just fine," she said and left the room.

"Duh, I could've told you that myself," I muttered under my breath as I lay back down. The mattress on my hospital bed was so stiff that, upon waking, it was impossible to distinguish it from the Formica floor until I opened my eyes. Imagining my cloud-like down comforter and the soft flannel sheets on my own bed only made my longing to return home that much more desperate. I closed my eyes, imagining that this was some kind of horrible dream and attempting to will myself safely back home to my own bed again. As hard as I squeezed my eyes shut, I was still in the same place when I opened them. Even though I felt like I was in a nightmare out of a real horror flick, this was no dream. Frustrated, I gave up on my efforts to go back to sleep on that plank they called a bed and accepted the fact that I was up for the day.

The hospital's protocol for patients going to breakfast made me feel like I was in the military. For some reason I'll never know, our floor always had to wait for the other floors to pass by before we were allowed to eat. As the other patients filed past, I would stick my index and pointer finger up and say, "World peace" (and this was while I was on the so-called 'standard' drugs). We aligned in single file, each awaiting their turn at the cafeteria. The military aspect to the breakfast process was oddly balanced by the way it was also like kindergarten. If anyone acted up, the nurses would snap them back to the end of the line. It found it humiliating and dehumanizing to be treated as though we were incapable children, while also being expected to comply like trained soldiers.

As I neared my chance at the food, I sighed sadly, wondering what bland and unappetizing breakfast they had prepared us that day. "What's wrong, Samantha?" A semi-nice nurse asked me.

"I don't want to be here, and I hate waking up at 5:30. My bed is as hard as a rock, and I really don't like strange people sleeping in the same room as me," I complained honestly.

"Well, I guess you told me!" She smiled, trying to be friendly, while completely ignoring my concerns.

I sat down with a slop of eggs, some greasy bacon, and a cup of coffee. The medicine seemed to have extinguished my appetite. Foods that I had always loved to eat just didn't taste good anymore. I had no desire to eat, and I only did so, because the nurses watched us when they took us to the cafeteria. If we refused to eat, they would make sure that we did. I could always feel the nurse's beady little eyes on the back of my neck, staring me down to make sure that I wasn't giving my food away or playing with it. To make things slightly less dull, I would always tell the guy who was serving the coffee to give me the one with caffeine in it. I don't know if it had any, but the way he pretended to get a certain pot for me felt like a little bit of special treatment in the midst of that hell hole.

We returned to our rooms after breakfast in the same single file line. Then, we would make our beds, take showers, and get ready for the day. The whole primping routine felt fairly pointless, as there wasn't anywhere to go or anyone to see. On top of which, we weren't even allowed to have most of the tools necessary for looking presentable. I asked the nurse why I couldn't have a blow dryer, and she said that someone might try to hang themselves with it. The hospital would not let us have any kind of sharp object or anything that the patients might be able to use to try to kill themselves. Also forbidden were shoelaces, as well as any makeup compact with a mirror. If a girl wanted to shave her legs, she was required to have a supervisor watching to make sure that she didn't try to cut herself. Someone was watching every single thing we did. I would call it an invasion of privacy, but there was no privacy to invade in the first place. I truly believe that the constant presence of someone watching over me, coupled with the cocktail of five different prescription drugs I was on, spurred the extreme paranoia that I developed during that time.

When we were finished with our ablutions, we would assemble into our groups. We were divided into the groups based on our behavior. If a patient was on her way out and didn't need much help, she would be in Group One. Someone who was close to being on her way out but who still needed some guidance would be in Group Two. Group Five, on the other hand, was composed of the patients who needed the most drastic aid. I was in Group Five. For the life of me, I couldn't understand why I was in that group.

We would move, as a group, through different classes over the course of the day. One class would be for stress relief, the next for coping skills, and so on. I was learning how to share and play nicely with the other kiddies, just like kindergarten all over again. Each class lasted an hour. Those hours dragged by tediously, each one seeming longer than the last. I'd watch the clock and await more drudgery. Though the counselors were nice, they seemed to be annoyed by me. I didn't understand why that was. Now, I'm not even sure if they were ever even annoyed with me after all. It could have all been a part of my drug-induced paranoia. There was no way to tell. To this day, I can't tell you what I might have learned from those 'classes'.

We were supposed to have gym class every day so that we could improve our health and emotional wellness through the benefits of physical exercise. However, the truth was that we rarely went to the gym. The staff would always have excuses as to why we were too busy for exercise. I figured they were just lazy. They were paid hourly so why exert themselves more if they didn't have to?

If we wanted to use the telephone to call someone, we could only use the pay phone. No cell phones were allowed. We could try to be sneaky, of course. Some patients would attempt to outsmart the system and have a visitor smuggle in a phone for them. This worked for a little while, but it was very difficult to conceal anything with so many eyes watching at all times. Anyone who had a phone while I was in there was caught eventually.

Visiting hours were held in the common area. They were only on certain days, and each patient was allowed a limited number of visitors at a time. My mom would be there every chance she got. In the beginning, Kathy would visit, too. Then, she and my mom had words, and she never showed up again.

My mom would bring me whatever she could. My two most requested treats were candy and cigarettes. Once I started taking the prescription medications, I began chain-smoking. I had only been a social smoker before, if that; but suddenly, I craved smoking and loved it. One time, my mom brought me candy, and the nurses took it away. They said that the hospital didn't want us to have it because they were afraid that we would give it to potential diabetics or that the sugar might keep us up at night. I heard those nurses snickering an hour later about how the candy they'd taken from me was the good stuff and they had enjoyed it. I also saw the wrappers from my candy on their counter. I thought this was needlessly evil of them. After that instance, I would put the candy in my bra and sneak it into my room.

In addition to all the eyes of the hospital staff that were on us, there were also some medical students from Wayne State University who were there to observe our behavior and progress. One of the female students would always dress in black, so naturally I was sure she was an FBI agent. Along with the plethora of irrational thoughts that had been invading my brain ever since I'd been taking all the prescriptions, I had begun to believe that the FBI was after me. My reasoning was that they knew I had too much information. It had been two years since 9/11, and I thought I knew that the terrorists were planning their next plot. I felt like I was somehow connected to the United States government and that I could telepathically communicate with them. My rationale was incredibly bizarre.

As I remained on the combination of five different prescription drugs, they continued to take their toll. I was never able to focus or concentrate. My eyesight was declining. I would blurt out words without prompting and speak when I wasn't supposed to. I felt as though I was reverting to my childhood ways, as if I were going backward in life instead of forward. It was a strange and very uncomfortable feeling to know that I had lost control so drastically. I was still somehow aware I had lost it and that that was why I was in there.

Upon reflection, I now believe more in nurture than nature as a result of my experiences in that hospital. The way I see it, if a completely normal person is put into an arena with a bunch of mentally ill people, that previously stable individual will eventually begin to feel mentally unstable, too. Even though the staff may be sane and normal, they're trained not to get too close to the patients. Thus, everyday life for any patient in such a place is made up of mentally ill people and their actions. In time, the stable person will likely come to be unable to decipher between healthy and unhealthy or between normal and abnormal because they're completely secluded from the outside world. They have no access to normalcy. We were not allowed to watch television or to know what was going on in society while we were in the hospital. The isolation intensified daily as the distance between us and any semblance of normalcy seemed to grow exponentially. Because of this, everything and everyone we saw was in a state of mental illness. When something surrounds a person in such a way, it can't help but rub off on them. The effects of such influences on our perception can be terrifying.

Chapter Eight

I never thought this could happen. For as long as I can remember, I always believed that our family would get through the rough patches. I couldn't fathom what was happening or even begin to voice the resulting feelings. My father had left us. He completely stopped supporting us, took off, and left all of the bills in my mother's name. She scrambled to try to find the money to stay afloat, but it was futile. We just didn't have the means to pay our bills. Before we knew it, the house was in foreclosure. My father's only attempt at alleviating the situation was to drive my mother to a women's shelter to get information on admitting my mom, my brothers, and me. We were desperate, devastated, and on our way to being officially homeless.

It felt like a knife had stabbed my heart and kept twisting and turning. The pain was too much for me to handle. I hated my father for this. I hated him so much that I fantasized about turning into a 10,000-pound gorilla and ripping out his fucking eyeballs. I wanted to murder the woman who (I thought at the time) had been the cause of our sudden destitution. I was so angry inside. It was as though my father had ripped out my heart and destroyed my soul. I was sad. I was embarrassed. I was infuriated. It was one of the hardest things I'd had to endure in my life so far.

Even more difficult than the fact that this was happening to me was the fact that it was happening to *us*. There were four other people experiencing the same whopping betrayal. I had never seen my mom so low. She was a wreck. This had all been abrupt and without warning, a slap in her face. The weight of it all was clearly taking its toll on her. When she wasn't crying, she would just stare blankly into an imaginary horizon.

With my dad out of the picture, the four of us were basically alone. My grandfather (Mom's dad) had died [**how long ago**]. My grandmother was still alive, but she wasn't my biological grandmother. She was my mother's stepmother, and the two of them were not on speaking terms with each other. Mom had never really been able to get along with her stepmother. When she was eleven years old, my mom's biological mother died of breast cancer. Her father worked two jobs just to keep food on the table. So, Mom was left to care for her four other siblings on top of taking on the responsibility of all the cooking, cleaning, laundry, and all the other chores for the entire household. A year later, my grandfather met who I now know to be my grandmother. She had seven children and was a widow. Before they knew it, my mom and her siblings picked up and moved in with my grandmother and her kids. Twelve children were then living together in one household. That's double the *Brady Bunch*. There were five girls and seven boys. Even back then, twelve kids was a big deal. The local newspaper would even write articles on them calling them 'cheaper by the dozen'.

The death of a mother and a sudden move to such a chaotic mishmash of a household would be traumatizing for any young girl. My mom spent the next few years bitter, sad, angry, and lost. It was so tough on her that she ended up moving in with her grandmother by the time she turned eighteen. She left with a ten speed, a change of clothes, and a major chip on her shoulder.

Through the years, my mother kept in contact with her father and some of her full siblings. My grandfather came to some school plays and music concerts, and we'd go to lunch often; but we rarely went over my grandparents' place. My grandfather would usually have to come and visit us at our house. It was sad for me because I wanted us all to be one big family. That didn't happen because my mother and her stepmother were always in conflict. My grandfather later passed away, and my mother and her stepmother didn't talk after that.

Despite the relationship that my mom had with my grandmother, I had a solid, loving relationship with Grandma. She and I were very special to each other. We had always kept in touch and made sure we spent time together. When Dad started to become more and more absent in our lives, I refrained from mentioning it to Grandma, because I didn't want her to worry. Meanwhile, the situation worsened to the point where we were on the brink of homelessness. When she took me out to lunch one day, I knew I had to tell her what was happening with our family. By the time the meal ended, I still hadn't worked up the nerve. We were waiting for the check, while I pushed uneaten food around on my plate. I'd never been very good at hiding things from Grandma, and I now know that she'd sensed something since the moment she saw me that day.

"Okay, Samantha. Now tell me what's wrong." She took me by surprise. I looked into her bright blue eyes as she folded her frail hands on the tabletop.

To me, Grandma was amazing. She was empathetic, generous, and the most devout Catholic I had ever met. She was always trying to do whatever she could to help others. Having Grandma was almost like having an older best friend, and I looked up to her as a person to whom I could confide. She always just knew what I needed to hear or when I needed her to listen to me. It was impossible to lie to her. Now that she'd opened the gates, the flood of emotions poured out of me. I looked at her and spilled my guts. I was bawling by the time I told Grandma that we might be going to a shelter because we had nowhere else to go. Once I'd finished telling my woeful tale, Grandma didn't miss a beat.

"You just leave everything to me." She spoke with a stern sympathy in her voice. "I will take care of everything; don't you worry a bit." I looked up at her, smiling slightly through my tears. She was wearing a lavender blouse that day, and it made her eyes look even bluer than they already were. Her confidence and sincerity seemed to glow through her. To me, at that moment, she looked like an angel.

"Okay," I replied, knowing then and there that everything would be all right.

I went home from lunch that day feeling strangely optimistic. I was just so thankful that someone cared about us. I'd been thinking that everything was crumbling and that our lives were at a dead end. It was as though it was thundering and lightning, and we were bracing ourselves for total devastation. Then, just in time, Grandma showed up, and the clouds began to part. It wasn't sunny yet, but I could see bits of light starting to peek through, thanks to her. It made me feel peaceful. I counted my blessings that day. Had she not come along, we would've been headed to a women's shelter. I was overjoyed that my grandmother, my angel, had rescued us from that bleak fate. That night, instead of tossing and turning with angst, worry, and fear; I actually slept soundly for the first time in weeks.

I was talking with my grandmother the next day when she asked me to put my mother on the phone. I gingerly handed the receiver to my mom. To my surprise, she took the call. She didn't smile or do so cheerfully, but it was a first that she even let Grandma talk to her. I watched my mother and listened. She didn't say much and just kept repeating, "Okay. All right. Mmm-hmm. Yes, okay." She was slumped on the edge of the couch, gazing out the bay window with a blank stare. Grandma was telling my mother that a moving truck would be there in a couple of days. She told her to pack as much as we could and that my cousins and uncles would handle the heavy lifting.

When my mom hung up the phone, she turned to look at me. Her blank stare gave way to a rush of tears. I think I held her for half an hour. We realized at that moment that we were fortunate to simply have one another. Someone my mother had once despised had become her ally. To me, it was a beautiful thing that finally brought our family some long-awaited relief.

I was still under a lot of distress, but deep down, in a part of my soul, I saw there was hope for us. Strange as it might sound, it ended up making me really happy that the whole thing had happened. This was the first time I had witnessed a seemingly doomed, frightening instance turn into something sacred and hopeful. My biological family was splitting up, but my family by marriage was coming to the rescue.

My grandma was truly an angel who saved us from going to a shelter. This angel was protecting us from the storm and making it sunny again, slowly but surely. I was flabbergasted. I was going to be all right; we were going to be all right.

Chapter Nine

The first time I went into the hospital, I was discharged within three days. I hated being there. Even after only a few days, I was ecstatic to be going home. That hospital felt like prison to me. The food stank, and the bed was hard. I was surrounded by crazy lunatics and mean nurses. There was nowhere for me to workout, and I only grew more depressed after I admitted myself. Now that I was back in the hospital again, I felt as though I was walking down some kind of trick hallway that got smaller and smaller and eventually just came to a point. I was stuck. There was no door through which I could escape, no emergency evacuation route, no safe word. I was trapped in a nightmarish situation that seemed to get worse by the minute. The longer I was there, and the further I went, the more trapped I became.

My aunt had said that this was the place to get help and that these doctors would help me get better. However, my experience was basically the opposite of what my aunt had expected. The minute I walked onto the floor where I would be staying, a nurse sprung over to me as if it were the highlight of her day.

"Samantha Lowe! Time to take your meds." She held out a white paper cup. Peering into it, I saw a bunch of strange pills that were huge and all different colors. I almost thought she was joking. No doctor had seen me. No nurse had diagnosed me. For all they knew, I could be there just to score drugs. I couldn't believe it.

"Excuse me, ma'am, but I don't even like to take aspirin for a headache. I am not taking those pills," I said. She didn't flinch.

"I'm sorry, but I am afraid you don't have a choice. You are under our care so what we think you need goes." I looked at her in horror. "Take the medication, Ms. Lowe, or I will call security." By this point, she was starting to get irritated with me. Her tone was quite fierce, and I was getting frightened. I wanted to acquiesce, but not knowing what the pills would do to me was scary.

"What are they?" I asked, as I had every right to know. She ignored the question.

"They are going to make you better. Now take the goddamn pills, or I will call security, and they will make you take them by holding you down!" She was getting angrier and angrier.

Out of duress, I decided to take them. I had to. I knew it was the only way to shut up the nurse and avoid a scene. With as much indignation as I could exhibit while also complying, I swallowed all four pills at once. Gulp. Gulp. Gulp. *Oh, shit*, I thought immediately. What were these things going to do to me? I was just taken to the emergency room in an ambulance for a bad reaction to a medication, and now I was taking more unidentified pills. What had I done? I thought about making myself vomit, but I knew that would only get me in trouble. What I didn't know at the time was that those little pills were only the beginning of a long, frightening nightmare full of pain and deception. I would soon have the kind of weird, terrifying, psychedelic mind trips that I'd only seen in the movies.

My frustration over the pills had caused my face to flush with anger. No sooner did the flush begin to fade did I start to feel incredibly drowsy. My vision began to get blurry. I was woozy and tipsy, like I'd just downed five stiff cocktails in a row. Then, I started to feel like I was being pulled toward the floor. Sure that I was going down, I headed to my room and collapsed onto the bed. I was conscious for long enough to recognize the same thin, hard mattress beneath me before I was sucked into a drugged unconsciousness.

Pop! Pop! Bang! Bang, bang, bang! I awoke in a panic and instinctively jumped out of my bed. I couldn't identify the sound I'd just heard, but it was loud enough to jolt me awake. It sounded like a gun or some kind of war noise. My instinct was to run, but my muscles were still sound asleep, and I felt as if I'd been tapped and drained of every ounce of energy. I was still engulfed in a groggy fog.

Through clouded vision, I could see there was another person sharing my room with me. Apparently, the privacy I'd had before had been too luxurious. Whoever was in the other bed must not have heard what I heard, for she was still out cold.

Suddenly, it occurred to me that I had no idea how long I had been asleep. Nor did I have any idea of what was happening. I felt very alarmed and frightened. Was someone shooting up the hospital? Concerned, I shuffled to the door and stepped out of my room. The woman in the room next to me slowly emerged from her room at the same time I did. "Did you hear that?" I asked.

"Yeeeaaaahhh." It took her at least four seconds to speak the one syllable word, and her looks resembled that of a zombie. Her eyes were droopy, and her speech was slurred. She stood hunchbacked and walked very slowly. We made our way to the lounge, where, to my surprise, everything looked completely ordinary. Patients were mingling around the television as usual; the floor was scattered with books. Nothing looked different. No one even seemed to notice us.

One might expect me to be relieved that nothing seemed to be awry, but that fact scared me even more. This meant that I was just hearing gun shots. I had only been on the medication for a couple of hours. What was that all about? I was checked into this place, medicated without being tested or diagnosed, and now I was hearing gun shots. That could not be good. The hospital reminded me of an assembly line at an automotive plant. *Grab. Insert. Swig. Swallow. Next!* This place was a factory for crazy people. Instead of, say, testing or examining the patients, they just simply checked them in and automatically started force-feeding them psychotropic drugs. Those without family or advocates were often just drugged and then left alone and ignored indefinitely.

I felt like something was gravely wrong with me, and the environment wasn't helping. I was incredibly upset but still overwhelmingly tired. I had to sit down. I found the closest chair and took a seat, trying as hard as I could to grasp where I was and what was happening. The chair was made of hard plastic and was almost harshly cold. Still, I felt myself sinking into it more and more. My body suddenly felt like it was morphing into the chair, like I was *becoming* the chair. It was nearly impossible to lift a limb off the chair or to push myself off it. It was as if the only direction to go was into the chair. I knew this was impossible, even though it seemed real to my brain at the time. I felt so out of it. I knew that I was now as crazy as anyone else in there. I had no control when I was in that hospital. The nurses and doctors and the medication were in control. I swallowed a handful of mystery pills and watched myself go from normal to zombie in a matter of minutes.

I wanted more than anything to go home right at that moment. This place was a far cry from the helpful haven my aunt believed it to be. As far as I was concerned, it was a prison. I couldn't leave if I wanted to. I had no rights. The nurses would second guess anything and everything I said to them, because they assumed I was crazy. It was a nightmare. I wanted out, and I wanted out *now*. I started to think not just of being home, but of everything I was missing with each passing day. I had been planning on taking my mom to an ice show. I had the tickets. Mom was looking forward to it. I knew then that I couldn't go. No one gets out of the hospital until they think you're ready to go. I wasn't even getting better. I was getting worse, and I knew it. I didn't know what to expect in the coming days or weeks. I had no idea when or if I would be released.

Just as I was getting agitated, the drugs took over again. I was on three different medications, and I was so loopy I didn't know what was going on half the time. The drugs seemed to work in shifts. One would go strong for a while, then I'd have a moment of clear thought, and then another one would kick in and take me in a completely different direction. My life and my body had been taken over by heavy-duty medication, and it was controlling everything: my thoughts, my mood, my motor skills, my future.

"Samantha, wake up." One of the only normal, nice nurses in there was an African American woman named Sharon who was thin with short curly hair. She woke me in her usual calm voice. "I have to take your vitals, and you keep falling asleep."

"What? What time is it? You'd be falling asleep, too, if someone woke you up this early." It was early morning again. I had been told this was a place where I could rest, but I wasn't getting much sleep at all. Sharon was very gentle as she took my vitals. She was careful not to poke and prod like some of the other nurses did. Even though it was five o'clock, I didn't mind her as much, because she was decent to me. "Now, breakfast will be starting shortly so make sure you get in line, Jessica."

I rolled over with a defeated groan. I was tired of getting in lines. I was sick of being in this hell hole. I yearned to be home again. I missed going outside. I missed sleeping in as late as I wanted to. I missed being able to get up in the middle of the night and going to the fridge for a simple glass of water. I missed my family. I missed freedom. I missed the lucidity of not being drugged up on God knows what medication. I was even more of a mess than I was when I walked through the door. *I should have listened to the ambulance driver*, I thought, *he was right*. He had been warning me to turn around; he was trying to tell me not to check myself in to this place. Those mental institutions pretend patients are there on their own free will, but that's not true. Once a person signs themselves in, it's not as simple as just signing themselves out when they're ready to leave. Patients sign their rights away when they check themselves in so there's no turning back until a doctor says they can leave. It was a trap, plain and simple.

It was getting to be Christmastime, and I was anxious about missing all the fun activities. For as long as I could remember, I'd looked forward to Christmas all year, every year. Would I have to spend the most wonderful time of the year in what felt like prison? I was terrified. I shuddered at the thought of spending the holiday in the loony bin with a bunch of people who I tolerated, at best. There was no way I wanted to remain in that morbid place for my favorite holiday. I wouldn't let that happen. I just wanted a comfortable bed, a pretty Christmas tree to look at, a warm, home-cooked meal, and some time with my mom and my two brothers. That was it. Was it so much to ask?

The longer I was on the drugs, the more I vacillated in and out of lucidity. I was not myself. The first time my mom came to visit me,

I was drooling, and my tongue was hanging out of my mouth. She looked at me horrified, sadness weighing in her eyes, almost like she was seeing me lying dead in a casket. I had never seen her that sad, not even at her own father's funeral.

"Samantha." She was holding back tears as she tried to spit it out, "I don't think you are going to be okay. You are not okay. I can't stand seeing you like this."

"Don't worry, Mom," I groggily pleaded. "I will be all right as soon as I get out of here. We'll spend Christmas together like a normal family, and everything will be all right. I promise I won't let myself take a turn for the worse." She looked at me with disbelief and nodded with tears still streaming down her face.

My appearance and demeanor must have been pretty crude and intense for her to get that upset. She was so torn up that her uneasiness was even startling me. Yet I knew that I was still there. Underneath those vicious drugs and the doctor's recent bipolar diagnosis, I was sure I was okay. So, I resolved to get out of there before Christmas, if it was the last thing I did. I decided to be on my best behavior. I would be good and obey. I would play the game that the nurses and doctors wanted me to play so that I could go home. It might not be easy, but I was determined to get better and come out on top in the end.

Chapter Ten

I didn't have to remain in the overnight stay unit for very long. I think it was only about three more days, though I can't remember for sure. My aunt and uncle invited me to stay with them and dedicated themselves to watching over me so that I would be allowed to come home. It was just before Christmas when I was released from the hospital. I was happy to be out and especially happy to be out in time for all the usual festivities. I would be able to go to church and see all the decorations around town. I could come home to a twinkling Christmas tree and all the embellishments that went with it. My evenings could now be spent curled up in the cozy living room, taking in the aromas of Christmastime cooking and baking that wafted from the kitchen.

What I wasn't looking forward to, was seeing people other than my immediate family. I was overjoyed to get to be with my mom and brothers, but I was pretty embarrassed when it came to seeing extended family and friends. I was frail at that point, and I was having a hard time eating, so it was impossible to gain any weight. A side effect of the medication I'd been taking was blurred vision. I had to wear a pair of flimsy, bifocal glasses that made my eyes magnify like *ET's* so I thought I looked ugly. My hair was perpetually greasy, dull, and stringy; which I believe was due to the general toxicity of so many medications constantly being pumped through my body. Overall, I just didn't look like me. Where I'd at least felt pretty decent looking before, I now saw myself as hideous.

On top of my appearance, the medications continued to have a significant impact on my mental and emotional state. I had developed a strange obsession with terrorists, along with a growing paranoia that the FBI was after me. Oddly enough, this is a known side effect of medications like those that I was prescribed at that time. Just like the intern from Wayne State I saw in the hospital, I thought every person in black was an undercover FBI agent and that they were following me. I swore I would see these 'agents' stick their finger in their ear to depress some kind of a button that allowed them to communicate with the other FBI agents and report my behavior. I was constantly anxious and fearful. If someone were to look at me a certain way, I would get scared. I felt like Tony Soprano or a celebrity with the paparazzi after them all the time. I was always looking around to see who was watching me. Every time I saw someone who looked suspicious to me, I would get so frightened that I felt I immediately needed to get out of there and hide. Even if I saw someone I knew, I would be suspicious of them and secretly try to determine whether or not they were an agent. I didn't have the ability to recognize others as simple, regular people. I was consumed by fear. I felt like a teeny tiny mouse on a huge planet, constantly scurrying around to try and find a hole or a crevice in which to hide. I was deeply afraid of acting out the part of the diagnosis I'd been given. I didn't want anyone to see me as a bona fide paranoid schizophrenic.

My mental state necessitated that someone monitor me at all times to ensure I didn't harm myself or another, or do something that would get me thrown back into the hospital. The need for a constant chaperone, in combination with my paranoia and impulsiveness, kept me cooped up in the house most of the time. Don't get me wrong—it was much better than being cooped up in the hospital, but I longed to go out and live the way normal people do.

When my aunt and uncle left town for a couple of days, my other aunt (on my father's side) came to 'babysit' me. Aunt Tara is a very unique person. Part Cherokee Indian, she has long, dark brown hair that goes to the middle of her back. She doesn't need to wear much makeup, because she's fortunate enough to be an elegant, natural beauty. She is very patient and has calm, beautiful brown eyes that seem to have the power to still and relax those who gaze into them. She is very sweet and giving by nature. I always received the greatest gifts from her at Christmas. She is very wise, and she seems to know at least a little bit about everything. She cooks like you can't believe, making nearly everything from scratch. You wouldn't guess that she is a mother of two boys because she acts calmly, as if she'd never even had children.

I could see the compassion that Aunt Tara had for me. She could tell I was doing my best, but that I longed for at least a modicum of normalcy. The two of us were in the kitchen catching up when she devised the best plan I'd heard in months. Instead of spending yet another day lazing around the house, we decided to take a trip into Kerrytown. Kerrytown is a historic market district in Ann Arbor, Michigan. I'd always liked Ann Arbor because of its quaint charm and its happening downtown area near the University of Michigan campus. Kerrytown was one of my favorite pockets of the city. I was fascinated by its history, which centered around three historic buildings built in the late 1800s. Back then, those buildings housed the lumber, warehousing, feed, and grain trades. In fact, the majority of the city of Ann Arbor was built with lumber hauled in horse-drawn loads from Kerrytown's Luick Bros.' lumber yard. Those three buildings have since been preserved, maintaining as much of their original integrity as possible, right down to the brick and exposed beams that characterized the original structures. I loved the look of those old-timey buildings that now held all kinds of shops, markets, and restaurants.

When we got to Kerrytown, I was so excited to be there. Just to be out of the house felt thoroughly rejuvenating. I had really missed feeling like a regular person. This outing was just what I needed. After doing a little browsing, Aunt Tara and I decided to stop and get some lunch. We chose a cute little Japanese sushi restaurant. It was so tucked away in a little corner of a bunch of stores that one could walk right past it without even realizing it was there. I was thrilled.

"Table for two, please," Aunt Tara said to the hostess.

We took our seats in a corner.

"I love Japanese food. They didn't serve it in the hospital," I said.

"Well, I would imagine they didn't. No fine dining there, huh?" she chuckled.

"What are you going to have?" I asked. "I like everything: tempura, sushi, stir fry ..." Another symptom of my condition was that it was so hard for me to make even a simple decision. I was always dissecting things and making them more difficult than they really were, always overanalyzing. After flip-flopping back and forth many times, I finally chose the shrimp tempura.

The waitress was a Japanese woman, who I suspected to be the owner, since she acted as both hostess and waitress.

"To drink?" she asked in delicate voice with an accent. Both Aunt Tara and I had the green tea. I was delighted to be sipping Japanese tea in a tiny, quiet restaurant with my lovely aunt in Kerrytown. I felt so much better at that moment.

"Thanks for taking me here. I really appreciate being able to get out and see things. I really love to eat at great places, and this one seems pretty neat." I had been used to cafeteria slop and food that was so bland it tasted like mashed air. I relished finally being able to enjoy a meal at a restaurant. I felt like I was actually starting to get my life back.

Then, with no warning whatsoever, a panic came over me. I was suddenly bombarded with anxiety, fear, and worry. My mind started racing for no apparent reason. Something had been triggered internally. My brain was receiving a message that I needed to be really freaked out, right then. I was having another panic attack. My heart was pounding a mile a minute. *Tha-thump, tha-thump, tha-thump!* I soon became riddled with anxiety to the point where I couldn't even think clearly. I had to slow my thought process down, but by the time I realized that, it was too late. I quickly put my napkin over my face.

"The vents!" I shouted. "They are filled with anthrax! The terrorists are trying poison us! Ahhhh! I can't breathe!" By that point, I was so scared, I was trembling. I couldn't sit still, and I kept spouting strange utterances.

A tall, thin Japanese man who was sitting across the room was watching me closely. He obviously didn't speak English, but he read my emotion. He soon followed suit and covered his mouth, as well. He must have thought I was normal and that I had a good reason for doing that. My panic attack had become contagious.

"What, Samantha? No, calm down. There is no anthrax. There are no terrorists here. We are safe. Please, just sit down, and relax. You are fine." I think my aunt felt bad that I was causing a major scene and getting a stranger excited for no reason.

I truly believed the terrorists had infiltrated the restaurant and were pumping anthrax through the heating vents. I was choking and acting as though I couldn't breathe. I was petrified, genuinely afraid for my life. I felt we were all in real danger and that it was imperative that I warn everyone immediately. My mind was racing again, like never before. I ignored my aunt's attempts to assuage my anxiety and instead ran outside with a napkin covering my mouth.

I had always believed that when people had panic attacks, they were just nuts. Not once in my life, prior to taking anti-depressants, had I ever had a panic attack. Now, I was drugged up and confused. It was as though my soul had found another body to inhabit. I felt like I was a person whom I had never met before, and I wanted her to leave as soon as possible. This person was not me. That was one of the most frightening moments—the moments when I wondered if I would ever get my real self back. I knew there were people who never came back from emotional states like the one I was experiencing. I refused to let that happen to me.

My aunt was remarkably good at keeping her cool. I don't think I saw her get stressed or even raise her voice. I do think she was slightly dumbfounded, though. She had never seen me this way before. To her, I was the brave and strong little niece she had known since birth. In fact, she used to love to tell me a story about when we were hit by a sudden storm when I was an infant. My mom and dad used to put me in a wooden bassinette when they would bring me over to Tara's. My uncle used to train horses for racing, so they lived on a farm with lots of land. One evening when she was babysitting me, my aunt decided to take a walk around the grounds with me in the bassinette. All of a sudden, a Michigan thunderstorm came tumbling down upon us. There was a torrential downpour, thunder, lightning, and even hail. She ran to the closest building, which was the barn. It had a steel roof so the sound of the balls of hail smacking the steel was jarring and frightening. Yet I didn't make a peep. She said she was so impressed by how calm I had been. It probably hurt her to then see me go from a composed little baby girl to a grown woman with such a loose grip on reality. I don't doubt that she feared I was permanently messed up, that I would be so for the rest of my life.

After a few moments, I just came down from the anthrax scare like nothing had happened. We went back to our meal without blinking an eye. After lunch, we left the restaurant and decided to explore Kerrytown. I liked the way it seemed that the people there remained true to their roots. The whole town had managed not to conform to corporate America and instead had kept the area to all mom-and-pop shops. There were a plethora of neat little stores, and there was a surprise in every nook. You could find just about anything there, if you looked hard enough. There was even a spot in the center of the shops where farmers would go to sell homemade honey, jams, jellies, crafts, and art pieces. I thought it was so cool. It made me feel very at home.

As we browsed, I came across a tall, fuzzy hat that I really took a liking to. It looked like a hat that a Russian person would wear in the winter, a babushka. I wanted to buy it. My aunt was so sweet that she bought it for me as a gift. I went on to wear the hat for the rest of the winter that year. Michigan winters can be brutal, but that hat kept me warm. I thanked my aunt profusely for the hat, and we strolled down the street looking for the next surprise.

We came to an intersection, and I felt my energy begin to heighten. It was coming back again; I was having another panic attack. However, this episode was an excessively *happy* one. I began skipping and laughing and clapping my hands, almost like a little kid. I started to sing 'We're off to see Wizard' from *The Wizard of Oz*. I ran the aisles of the tiny, local grocery store; singing aloud. I remember people smiling at me. They must have thought I was either crazy or on some really intense drugs. By that point, Aunt Tara was getting used to my behavior. She kept her calm and seemed completely fine with how I was acting.

"Hey," she said. "I guess this is the best place for you to do this. The people here won't mind." Ann Arbor is a very open-minded city where people aren't afraid to let others state their opinions or be whoever they want to be, and I was doing just that. All I remember about the rest of that episode was that I purchased an odd mix of items at the grocery store, including a beautiful rose that I gave to my aunt as a gift. Then, as we were finishing up at the register and leaving the store, the attack subsided just as quickly as it has come on.

I would go from high to low and back to high, just like that. Presto-chango! One moment, I was as still as a statue; and the next moment, I was bouncing off the wall like a rubber ball. It was so uncontrollable that when the highs came on, it was as though another being had commandeered my body and taken for me a wild, uncontrollable ride.

We decided to leave Kerrytown after the second episode. My aunt had to stop at the supermarket to pick up some groceries. She parked the car, and as I stepped out, I felt another panic attack coming on again, number three for the day.

"They're coming!" I began to shriek. "The terrorists are coming after us! They are going to attack again!"

"Samantha, honey, settle down. There are no terrorists at the store. You are safe; I won't let anything happen to you." She was so gentle and calm throughout these panic attacks, it almost seemed like they didn't even faze her.

"Arrghhh! Over there!" All of a sudden, I saw a clown coming towards me. I was terrified of clowns. "The clown is over there! It's a clown face and he is coming after me! Get him away! Get him away!" I was frenzied. There was no clown. It was a winter day, and there was snow on the ground. I was hallucinating, and I had seen a clown's face coming out of the snow, as if someone put it there on purpose in order to scare me. The medication I was on was so powerful that I actually saw that imaginary clown with my very own eyes.

"Samantha, there is no clown, and there are no terrorists. Please calm down."

Just then, I saw a man out of the corner of my eye. He looked as though he was of Indian or Arabic descent, which gave me the idea that he might have been the mastermind behind the clown trick. I was sure he had a gun.

"He's going to shoot me!" I looked at him with terror and hit the ground in a flash. I was so terrified that this random man was out to get me. I grabbed my cell phone and dialed 911. I was going to tell the police I had a terrorist after me and that he had a gun. My aunt's composure cracked for the first time all day. I saw the fear come over her, the look of deep concern that I would never be normal again. I wanted to console her, to snap back to my real self, but I had no control. I put the phone up to my ear as it started to ring on the other end.

"Samantha, no! Don't call the police! Hang up!" My aunt was stern as she was frightened that I would make a false accusation to the authorities. She then forcefully grabbed the phone out of my hand. What I didn't realize at the time was that she was saving me from going back to the hospital. If I would have reached the police and made a false report, they would've had grounds to readmit me.

"Everything is okay," Aunt Tara spoke into the phone. "She is fine, I am sorry for the mishap." She shut the phone and put it into her pocket. "Samantha, no one is after you. You are fine. There are no terrorists around here, and there is no reason to call the police like that! You are hallucinating. Calm down, and let's go shopping, I have to get a few things for dinner."

Bewildered, I followed her into the store like a lost puppy. My own behavior was terrifying me. Had I lost my mind? Was I really going to be like this forever? Were the drugs overpowering my well-being? I was not in control, and I missed the old me. I missed the strong and smart woman I had been. I was hopeful I would be able to snap out of this soon. I couldn't take it anymore. The panic attacks put so much stress on my mind and body that I was afraid they would give me a heart attack. The paranoia was taking me over to the point where I didn't even feel I could go five minutes without being fearful that someone was watching or coming after me.

Thankfully, that was the last time my aunt had to save me from an episode. She was very good at helping me along the way. Through it all, she held my hand. She never gave up on me, and she was determined to help me. Others ignored the problem and didn't even want to see me that way. That was okay, too. Still, to have someone there for me who cared so deeply felt incredibly comforting. Between my family and my aunts and uncles, I knew I had a team of people who loved me and were rooting for me. It gave me hope and the inspiration to keep fighting. Their support made me even more determined to one day find myself again. This was not going to be easy, but I was never one to give up.

Chapter Eleven

Before I was first admitted to hospital, I'd had a boyfriend. We were still together when everything went down with me, though he was out of the country on an internship at the time. I won't use his real name for legal reasons, but let's call him 'Joe'. Joe and I met at U of M. I was at a party thrown by my roommate's brother. There was a weird guy there who kept hitting on me. He wasn't taking my hints, and he was growing creepier by the minute. Finally, out of despair, I spotted Joe and asked him to help get the guy to leave me alone. He did. Joe was handsome and very smart. He was getting ready to graduate from the University of Michigan and had started applying for law schools. We had a couple of drinks, and I asked him a silly question.

"If I had cancer, would you still like me?"

He replied with an affirmative.

The next week, he was my boyfriend.

Joe needed someone to love him, and I felt sorry for him. Growing up, Joe had been thrown in and out of boarding schools in Canada. His rich father couldn't be bothered to deal with him, and his mother was an alcoholic and manic depressant. When we met, Joe was recovering from a drug addiction, though I never knew which drug it had been. Joe had been with me since before my first incident, and he'd stayed in the relationship throughout all of it. I visited his family, and he was close with mine. He seemed like the perfect guy in many respects, and it looked like he'd actually turned out all right despite his family drama.

As we started hanging out more and more, I began to have no time to myself. Joe would only want to hang out with his friends, and he didn't seem to like any of my friends. I was forced to hang around people with whom I really didn't click. Joe's friends were hippies who liked to smoke pot and play Frisbee golf. That was not at all my scene. Always wanting to please, however, I pretended to enjoy them. He was also a bit of a control freak. I would come home from wherever I had been, and Joe would be waiting for me outside my door. It happened so frequently that it irritated my roommate and prompted her to question whether he even had a home. He just never wanted to be without me. On top of that, he always had to be in charge of what I said and did. Needless to say, I was not the perfect girlfriend, but I never cheated on him or did anything to warrant his mistrust. He was just suspicious—and, therefore, controlling—by nature. I attributed his idiosyncrasies to his past, though, and still felt he had a good heart. So, I stayed with him.

After graduation, Joe decided to study foreign trade law. With the help of his father, he obtained a coveted internship and went to work at the BMW corporate headquarters in Mexico for an entire semester. When he left, I was doing fine emotionally and was head over heels for him. My initial hospitalization occurred not long after he'd gone to Mexico. I knew my circumstances would be devastating to him. To make matters worse, I found out his mother had been treated for depression at the very same hospital. I felt horrible when I realized that, as I was sure he would be forced to relive the horrible memories he had of that time with his mother. I couldn't imagine how my own mother felt seeing her daughter this way. Yet to see your

mother like that, someone you are supposed to look up to and take advice from, had to be deeply frightening. From what I can remember, the first look Joe gave me when I was out of the hospital was one of disgust. I didn't see any sympathy, love, or relief on his face as I had hoped. Instead, I saw fear. He looked as though he was ashamed or even embarrassed.

The drugs did blur my perception and memories, but I do recall a specific incident that happened soon afterward. While I was in the outpatient day program, I let Joe use my leased vehicle. One day, he picked me up with an accusatory sneer.

"I cleaned your car, today … and I found something very interesting." He pulled a card from his pocket and shoved it in my face. I didn't even recognize it. "What is this? Whose number is this? Whose business card!?" He became overly agitated before we even left the hospital parking lot. It was so alarming that I was hoping someone would notice and come to my rescue by telling him to settle down. No such luck. I looked at the card and tried to reason with him.

"How would I know? I've been out of commission for weeks. All I know is that I don't know who it is, nor do I care right now. Please, just drive me home." I can't remember how the conversation went from there, but I do remember it was a tension-filled ride back to my aunt and uncle's. Joe was so insecure that he was always accusing me of things I hadn't done or even considered doing. It was unnecessary and very irritating. I wasn't in the state of mind to handle it, and I shouldn't have had to put up with such behavior. Instead of being there for me, it seemed like he was always finding reasons to push me further and further away. It was definitely working! I was frustrated.

A few weeks later, it was New Year's Eve, which is usually one of my favorite nights of the year. That year held a special significance, as I was looking forward to celebrating letting go of the old and looking toward what would hopefully be a much brighter future. Joe and I were cooking up a feast at my aunt's when my close friend, Maria, called.

"Hey, Jen, I know you aren't going out tonight. We're just going to lie low over here so I thought you might want to come by and just hang out." I thought that sounded perfect, so I asked her to hold on while I asked Joe.

"Joe, would you mind if we went to see my friend Maria after dinner? I haven't seen any of my friends in a while, and I think it would be good to get out and get some fresh air." I was so excited, I had been isolated for so long, and it felt as though Joe had been smothering me.

"Absolutely not. I am not going to hang out with your friends. Tell her no!" He was furious I had even asked such a question. I told her we wouldn't be able to make it without mentioning why not. I was totally embarrassed. Weeks later, Maria ended up telling me she knew what he'd said because she'd heard him.

Instead of going out to celebrate with friends, Joe and I stayed in with a rented video. I can't remember the details, but I think it was a suspenseful film where Robin Williams actually played a serious role. Mid-way into the film, a character started to flip out. He became agitated, got nervous and scared, and started shouting. I was still so sensitive and fragile that when he started to flip out, I became frightened along with him. I felt his pain and suffering, and became truly scared, too. I began to think someone was after me. I thought people could see me through the window, as if I were a part of the movie. I immediately shut all the shades and went into panic mode. I started screaming, yelling, and crying. I was a complete mess. I was genuinely terrified, and it was only a movie. We had to turn it off, and Joe ended up calming me down somehow. I had ruined my New Year's Eve.

The real scare that finally convinced me to break up with Joe happened when I accidentally forgot my pills one day when Joe was driving me to the day program.

"Uh-oh … oops!" I gasped.

"What now, Samantha? What is it?" I could tell that I was irritating him again.

"I forgot to take my pills this morning," I confessed. "I didn't do it on purpose," I said defensively. He threw his hands in the air and slammed them down hard on the steering wheel as he went off on me.

"What!? How could you? You know you have to take them everyday. How can you forget? Are you that dumb?! You can't even do something as simple as taking your medication?" He was yelling by that point.

I was so scared by his reaction that I believe his outrage triggered a minor mania for me. At that moment, we turned a sharp curve that revealed a congested strip of highway ahead of us.

"Look over there!" I pointed at the traffic. "It's the end of the world! You see all of those people in their cars? They're trying to get out of the city so that the terrorists don't get them! You see that! Look!"

I was screaming now. I was screaming nonsensical things that were not true. It was as though I was a child who couldn't help but get so worked up and excited. It felt like I was having a temper tantrum. Had I not been in the car, I likely would've kicked and screamed on the ground. It was horrifying to live like that. I couldn't be normal, no matter how hard I tried. The medications were controlling my mind and dictating my thoughts. Had I been all right, I would have known it was a simple traffic jam, that's all, not the end of the world.

This was just one of the many incidents I remember, though I know there were plenty more. I knew then that it just wasn't safe for me to be around Joe. Being in such a vulnerable state and so prone to upset, I needed to be nurtured and coddled; not judged and accused. I clearly wasn't able to handle the added stress of having to walk on eggshells around someone who was supposed to be supporting me. I finally began to realize that Joe being in my life was far more destructive than it was healing.

I remember telling the counselors at the day program about how he treated me. There were also a couple of friends in the group to whom I leaked such personal information. They all agreed it was time to call it quits. Though I had truly believed I was in love with Joe, I came to understand I was mostly just consumed by the concept of being in love. I had wanted that very feeling so badly for so long. I was desperate to have a long relationship, get engaged, and plan my wedding. It was so much more appealing to believe that he was 'the one' than to admit I was just lonely. At that point in my life, I needed to stay away from my worries and to pull through my sadness and sorrow. This was my time to grieve, get over it, and move on. It would be detrimental—and possibly dangerous—for me to be around someone who wanted to control me when I had little control of my own emotions and thoughts. This is what allowed me to finally be able to say goodbye to Joe and to brave my challenging path to recovery without him.

Chapter Twelve

I saw various doctors daily while I was in hospital. Still, it seemed like no progress was ever made. I didn't feel any better; my departure never seemed to get any closer. Even though I was there to recover and get help, I didn't feel I was getting the treatment I required in order to get better. However, when I would express that sentiment, the doctors would tell me that the more I talked, the more time I would spend there. That only made me feel worse. As this hell that was supposed to be temporary began to seem much more permanent, I searched desperately for distractions. Anything that could pull my focus was worth looking into, if only to pass a few moments of that bleak existence. Naturally, the most interesting part about the entire experience was the population of other people in there with me. I figured that as long as I had to be there, I might as well make the most of it. So I befriended who I could and studied the rest.

At one point, I had a roommate whose actual name I don't remember, but I'll call her 'Mary'. Despite the fact that she was close to fifty years old, she somehow resembled Linda Blair in *The Exorcist*. She snickered a lot, and her behavior was so unpredictable that I could actually imagine her shouting gibberish and projectile vomiting green pea soup like that possessed character. She was on the chunky side and had dingy brown hair that was stringy and went down to the end of her back. She seemed a little greasy overall, as if she always needed a shower. Her eyes were dark brown and squinty. She spoke with a very high-pitched voice that had a slight rasp to it. Her breathing was heavy and strained, possibly because of her weight. One rarely caught a glimpse of Mary in anything other than her ubiquitous yellow sweater with the sleeves rolled up to her elbows. She was on a ton of meds. Whenever it was time for medication, she would receive a heaping handful of God-knows-what.

One day, she would say nice things about me; and the next, she'd want nothing to do with me. I surmised that she was definitely either bipolar or schizophrenic. Either way, her illness was severe. She used to tell me her name was something other than Mary. She'd come up with different aliases all the time. One of the personas that stands out in my memory is 'Katherine Bates, mass murderer'. The fact that she believed herself to be that person was just as frightening as it would've been had it been true. Needless to say, sharing the same room with someone like her was more than a little unnerving.

I learned quickly that inventing stories and making fantastic claims is standard behavior for people who are mentally ill. It's difficult to determine whether or not they're telling the truth. Mary loved to talk. She would tell me strange things on a daily basis. She'd say, for instance, that she had a lot of money in the bank and that she was contemplating what to do with it once she got out of there. She'd go on to tell me that if I was smart and good enough for her, she would even consider giving me some. Luckily, I never believed her.

The more time I spent with Mary, the more she began to drive me up the wall. She would constantly hide my stuff and laugh to herself while I tried to find it. It wasn't at all funny to me because she would always choose to hide something I really needed. She'd steal my shoes or my toothbrush, for example. Or she'd somehow make off with the robe I wore day in and day out. What she considered a hilarious prank quickly got old to me. What added to her amusement—and my dismay—was the fact that when I would tell the nurses that my belongings were missing, they wouldn't believe me! They thought I was making it up for attention. Mary would eventually admit privately that she wanted to find out how smart I was by seeing how long it took me to find the objects she'd hidden.

I didn't like her at all back then. Now that I look back on it, though, I feel deeply sorry for her. I have no idea how long she had been there or whether she's been released since. How can anyone live their whole life like that, with their mind constantly out of whack and clouded by medicine? Thinking such crazy thoughts and going from high to low and back to high by the minute is unbearable. Think about how horribly overwhelming it can be to feel a huge amount of stress. Luckily, those of us with healthy mental functions have the ability to combat that stress with tools like exercise, music, or breathing. We have ways of calming our minds and refocusing on something else. Now, imagine having no control whatsoever over your mind and then feeling a ton of stress to boot. It is hellish.

I don't know if Mary had any family. For as long as we shared a room, no one came to visit her. When she wasn't occupying herself with pranks or tall tales, she was always moping around. I bet she just could have used someone to love her; someone to be there for her and tell her she was going to be all right; someone to help her pull through so she could be okay again. I don't know what happened to her. I pray for her in hopes that she made it out of the facility and that someone in her life was able to help her the way my mom and family helped me.

Another roommate of mine was an African American woman, who we'll call 'Sunny'. I'm giving her that name, because she was the most positive person I have ever met. The thing that amazed me about Sunny was her spirit. She was someone who made the best out of what life had handed to her. She had no fingers and barely any teeth left, yet she was as happy as could be. Of course, there were things she couldn't do with her hands, but she managed to do what she could. She found a way to brush her teeth and to comb her hair, for example. I never knew why she was in there. Aside from her physical disabilities, she seemed to be in decent shape.

Sunny was helpful to me. She truly cared about me, even though I barely knew her. When I would cry at night, she would whisper, "It's all right, Jessica. You are going to be okay. Trust me. I can see that you are bright, and I know that this is just a minor setback for you." It was incredibly comforting and endearing to have such a gentle, optimistic friend in a place like that. Unfortunately, I only got to stay with Sunny for a little while before they transferred me to another woman's room.

My next roommate was a fabulous pianist. Let's call her 'Gwen'. She was about 5'8" and heavy set. In no way was Gwen physically fit. Her body was soft and mushy, and she moved with visible effort. She had frizzy, blondish-brown hair that went to her waist, just like Mary's. Her light blue eyes emanated sadness. Gwen was Russian and barely spoke a word of English. Our only method of communication was through hand gestures and facial expressions. It was like living with someone who was deaf. I quickly had to become hyper aware of my emotions and facial expressions. Because she was mentally ill, she would get upset easily and start worrying if she saw something on my face that upset her.

We had a piano in our recreation room, and she played it beautifully—with expertise, in fact. She would play a song over and over again until every note was perfect. I truly enjoyed listening to her play. She would even give me mini lessons every now and then. She taught me how to sit up straight on the edge of the bench while playing. I learned where to position my hands and which fingers to use for which keys. I had played keyboard as a little girl. Back then, I would hear parts of songs and just play them by ear. In the hospital, however, I was not at all good at playing the piano. Perhaps it was another side effect of the medication. Maybe it was because I was just bored and trying to learn something to make the most out of my time in the hospital. My lessons with Gwen were short ones that ultimately ended with her getting frustrated and just walking away.

When we weren't playing the piano, Gwen would copy everything I did. If I combed my hair; she combed hers. When I threw my hands in the air; so did she. She thought it was a funny game. I suppose it was her way of playing with me, but having your every movement aped could drive anyone batty. I was no exception.

Gwen's illness manifested in its own, unique ways. She would often grab her stomach and rub it, as if she were pregnant. Since I couldn't ask her, I had no way of knowing whether she actually was, though I doubted it. She would hold her stomach, patting it while gazing lovingly at it. I finally had to know, so I asked the nurse if Gwen was with child. The nurse told me that she absolutely was not. She said it was just part of her illness and that she was hallucinating.

I felt terrible for Gwen when I heard that. It had to be awful to think that you have a living being inside of you, that is a part of you, and for that not to be true. I kept thinking of all the love and excitement and anticipation she must have been feeling and how it was all just a fantasy.

Despite the fact that we spoke completely different languages, Gwen and I still managed to argue sometimes. We both had strong, domineering personalities so it was pretty much inevitable. She would play the piano too loud, and it would annoy me. Or, she would be on it all day when I wanted to play. It was not much different than two children fighting over toys. In hindsight, I understand that the piano was Gwen's whole world while she was in the hospital. Since she couldn't speak English, she had no idea what was going on most of the time. She could really only experience her life in the hospital through eyesight and touch. It was sad.

Gwen's mother would visit her often. She was an attentive mother, caring and cute in her own way. Even though she didn't speak English either, she'd always smile at me and wave hello. I found it a little funny that, regardless of the temperature, she constantly dressed as though it were cold outside. She'd come to the hospital bundled up, always with some kind of hat pulled over her short, curly brown hair. She was chubby, too, but she was much shorter than Gwen. They would speak to each other in Russian, always talking very loud and fast. Even though I couldn't understand the language, it seemed that Gwen's mother would get frustrated with her at times. From their tone and gestures, I gathered that she wanted Gwen to just snap out of her illness and be okay.

I was thankful she had a mother who cared for her so much that she spent every possible visitor hour with her daughter. There was an incredible amount of sadness and compassion in her mother's eyes as she looked at Gwen. She wanted to see her daughter get better, to see her succeed. She longed for Gwen play the piano in front of others so that they could enjoy her beautiful music. No one could hear her play when she was in the hospital, and no one really cared in there, either.

Gwen's mother was not going to give up on her daughter. She was her number one fan.

I think about Gwen every now and then, and I can still see her face: her sad eyes, her gentle slight smile, and her innocence. I never found out what was wrong with her, but there is a part of me that thought she was just going through culture shock. Maybe she had a bad life in her country and saw horrible things that were bottled up inside her. She might have been raped or abused. Whatever the case, there was a child in her who wanted to be a woman living a life of music and peace. She seemed capable of making it and wind up okay. I hope she did.

My best friend in the hospital was a girl who we'll call 'Maggie'. Maggie saw me the second time I was admitted to the in-patient ward, when I'd had a panic attack in the day program. That time, they were about to put me on the floor that was half female and half male. Unfortunately, I blew my chance for that when I went through a mania of highs and lows as I was filling out my paperwork. When I was taking inventory of all my personal belongings so that they could confiscate any that were potentially harmful, I suddenly felt so violated and uncomfortable. I was a sad person having a completely normal reaction, and I was having my possessions taken away from me. Happy or sad, I wasn't a person who would ever try to commit suicide. I grew very upset, very quickly, which propelled me into the throws of my massive mood swings.

As I was checking in my life to a stranger, I noticed a man and a woman talking. They were so familiar and comfortable with one another that I figured they were brother and sister or at least good friends. My rambunctious behavior had caught their attention. I was talking loudly, saying anything that came to my mind.

"All you need is laughter and happiness!" I shouted and promptly followed up with, "We all need to leave here; they are using us just like lab rats!"

The woman stared at me, making direct eye contact. I screamed, "Ahhh-ha! I knew you were a nice person! I like you!" Her man friend didn't say a word. He was shocked at my behavior, despite the fact that it was commonplace for a mental hospital. After that, I would run into that woman frequently in the smoking hut outside. I found out her name was Maggie, and we became friends. I might have been in a fit of mania when I met her, but I'd known I liked her from the start. We were friends because we could relate to one another. She had scraggly, curly hair, fair skin and big brown eyes. I never knew what her illness was but she was just like me.

Mental facilities instruct their patients not to make friends or start love affairs with other patients. Because of this, I don't know where any of those people are today. Before I met these individuals, I used to be amused by people with mental issues. I saw it as though I was laughing with them. Now, I know that sort of behavior is affected by drugs or some kind of trauma or damage to the brain. Since I know how agonizing it can be, I don't find it funny anymore. While in the hospital, I prayed hard every night for the people in there with me and for myself. I still pray for them today with hopes that they, too, are living the good lives they all deserve.

Chapter Thirteen

I had always known that drugs were bad. Of course, everyone has heard that street drugs are bad, but I never even liked the way I felt after taking a simple aspirin or ibuprofen. Every drug, street or otherwise, has a unique effect on each person. The effects of some drugs vary slightly, while the effects of others can be drastically different depending upon the individual. The minute we start combining drugs, the effects are exponential. There are so many stories of celebrities dying from combinations of FDA-approved, doctor-prescribed drugs. Michael Jackson, Elvis, and Anna Nicole Smith are among the cases we've heard about, while there are countless others we haven't. When one person is taking many different kinds of medication, it's difficult for even the most conscientious doctor to keep track of all the possible harmful interactions. And there I was, hospitalized for normal depression, with all kinds of nurses and doctors—who weren't always communicating with one another—handing out pills like they were candy. Actually, our candy was far more closely monitored in the hospital than our medications ever were.

The pill cocktails and dosages I was given varied constantly so it's impossible to know how much of each drug I took at a time. In addition to the drugs I was prescribed to treat my symptoms, I was also prescribed drugs to offset the side effects of the other drugs.

For example, I was once given a drug to stop me from having seizures. Normally, I was at no risk of having a seizure. Yet it was perfectly acceptable to put me on a combination of pills that could result in my body reacting that way. I'm not a doctor, but I still can't help but feel that a seizure might be your body's way of rejecting certain drugs, or the combination of those drugs. The amount of medication and all the possible effects are a lot to wrap one's head around, but I'll share just a few of the medications I was taking.

The seizure medication was called "Oxcarbazepine", which is a generic for the brand name drug, Trileptal. It is a medication that is used to treat seizure disorders, of which it names epilepsy, specifically. Of the possible, typical side effects listed in the accompanying pamphlet, I experienced: dizziness, drowsiness, dry mouth, and constipation. Those are the side effects that one should contact their doctor about if they *persist*. There are other warnings in the pamphlet that instruct that one notify their doctor *immediately* if they experience any "unlikely but serious" side effects. From that list, I was experiencing vision problems, loss of coordination, trouble walking (downstairs only for me), and mood changes. Luckily, I escaped the bloody diarrhea and coffeeground vomit side effects of that one.

The next drug was Clonazepam, the generic for brand name "Klonopin". This medication is used to treat seizure disorders or panic attacks. The pamphlet warns about the dangers of not taking this drug exactly as directed and at the exact same time each day. It also warns about it being habit-forming while also losing its effect over time. Some of the more disturbing side effects of Klonopin include excessive hair growth or loss of hair, sore gums, unusual eye movements, increased salivation, rash, and trouble breathing. My bundle of side-effects from this drug included: a change in appetite (I couldn't eat), drowsiness, dizziness, fatigue, weakness, mood changes (drastic ones, in my case), blurred vision, weight changes (I looked anorexic), hallucinations, loss of coordination and difficulty speaking. Just looking back and recounting this now is scary! The pamphlet also instructs that a doctor be notified of all other medications you're taking, especially certain antidepressants and anti-seizure medication. Well, the last one I described, Oxcarbazepine, is an anti-seizure medication.

The next drug I was taking is called "Benztropine"; "Congentin" is the brand name. It's used to treat symptoms of Parkinson's disease or involuntary movements due to the side effects of certain psychiatric drugs. So this drug was also given to me to offset all of the side effects of all the other junk they were giving me. This is where I really start to feel like a lab rat. The pamphlet for this drug warns that it might take a few weeks or months "before the full benefits of this medication are observed". It also instructs not to stop taking this medication without doctor's approval, because stopping it suddenly "can sometimes lead to worsening symptoms". The side effects I got to enjoy with this drug were: drowsiness, dizziness, loss of appetite, vision changes, and sleeplessness. I also ended up with dry mouth, another known side effect for which they recommend sucking on (sugarless) hard candy or ice chips, chewing (sugarless) gum, drinking water or using saliva substitute. Gross. Still, this one was not as bad as the others.

"Risperidone" is the generic name for Risperdal. It's used to treat psychotic or mental conditions. Of the listed side effects, I had the following: drooling, mental confusion, seizures, loss of appetite, vision changes, and confusion. I was glad, though, that I wasn't a man taking this one. Its pamphlet includes the following warning: "Males- in the unlikely event you have a painful prolonged erection, stop using the drug and seek immediate attention or permanent problems could occur." Jeesh!

The doctors kept telling me to wait and give the meds time to "sink in". They told me that my body just had to adjust. Then, when a drug would be too overpowering for me, they would give me another one to replace it, and I would start the vicious cycle all over again. It was a never-ending battle. The interactions were dangerous, and the side effects far outweighed the positives, more often than not. This got me wondering what are the positives really were, anyway. For me, it didn't seem like there were any. At that time, I was depressed and sad without the medication, but I was an absolute mess with no ability to control my mind or emotions with it. I had never felt so horrible in my entire life, nor have I since. I wouldn't wish any of these symptoms or side effects on my worst enemy.

Now, I haven't studied every case of anyone who has ever been prescribed drugs. I only know my own experience and what I witnessed firsthand from inside that hospital. It's possible that drugs may be the answer for some people. However, they were clearly not the answer for me, especially not in that dosage or combination. The more and more I saw other people get hooked on these meds, I began to see worse and worse side effects.

As I observed this, what confused me was why the hospital was so hesitant to do the work it took to diagnose conditions before dolling out the medications to treat them. I mentioned in an earlier chapter that I was medicated before ever being given any tests. Once I was given those meds, my behavior instantly became disturbing and unpredictable. To look at me, one would naturally have assumed that I was mentally ill. However, no one got to look at me when I was off of the meds completely. There was a time when I requested that I be given an MRI in order to accurately diagnose my so-called schizophrenia. I was sick of taking the medication and being hospitalized. All I wanted was a routine test to show me the proof. When I asked the doctor, she refused, as she always did. I grew agitated so they immediately shot me up with Depacote—as they always did. I then went right back to being a drooling zombie without the mental function necessary to realize that a true diagnosis might be in order and demand one.

That was how I came to understand that the hospital was a gold mine. It was essentially a racket to milk insurance companies. My mother's attorney predicted my release, early-on. She said, "Just wait. Be patient. Let the insurance run out, and she will suddenly be ready to be released." That's exactly how it ended up happening, too. Conveniently, they never actually had any real proof that I was ever that sick. So when it came time to release me, they didn't have to provide any proof that I'd recovered.

Chapter Fourteen

When they finally let me out, I was transferred from in-patient care to the day program. Though I was ecstatic to be able to go home, I was still on all kinds of meds, still a complete wreck. I wasn't myself at all. I'd talk in circles, often losing track of what I was trying to say. My speech was slow, listless. I was definitely a far cry from the happy-go-lucky Samantha of the past. Because I felt so strange and confused, I was often quiet and withdrawn. I spent my evenings and off days not doing much of anything.

Even though I was officially an out-patient, I still ended up spending most of my time at the hospital. The insurance company had funds left to milk so they made sure I was there from 8 a.m. to 4 p.m. every day. The downside to not staying at the hospital was that I had no room there, which meant I had no privacy whatsoever. I was bombarded by people all day long. There were in-patients, outpatients, and many different nurses and social workers. The constant assault of being surrounded by people with no reprieve quickly grew irritating, while the routine soon grew tiresome. The doctor still saw me and made observations. I didn't know what she was writing in her notes, but I was sick of fighting the battle. I wanted to just be okay again. I was ready to get off the meds and get my life back, so I endured treatments all day, went home to sleep, and did it all over again the next day.

Aside from being able to sleep in a real bed at night, the good part of the day program was that there were some nice nurses there. One of my favorite nurses, Ms. Carol, was a complete sweetheart. Ms. Carol had short, wispy hair and eyes that were truly angelic. She never raised her voice or got angry, and she genuinely listened to what people had to say. I could tell her efforts were sincere. She genuinely wanted to help people recover. It was evident that she put all of her heart into what she did. I felt more at ease when Ms. Carol was around. I felt safe and as though I was treasured, similar to how I'd felt around my grandmother. I missed that feeling incredibly, so I spent time with Ms. Carol whenever I could. Despite the fact that nurses weren't supposed to get close to the patients, I got to know a little bit about Ms. Carol personally. She told me she'd been learning the guitar, and she also told me she had cancer. It was rare for a nurse to open up to the patients that much, and the fact that she did gave me a sense of normalcy, if only for that moment.

For me, the worst part of the day program was the fact that others were in there, some of whom didn't like me. There were other patients who thought I was annoying. Because I was still on all the meds, I was extremely emotional. To make matters worse, I was always talking. I couldn't shut up for the life of me. I would constantly speak out of turn, spouting anything that came to my mind. Being that it was a classroom setting, I was, in fact, being rude. The other patients' annoyances were justified. Sometimes, I would try to stop myself, but the meds were stronger than I was. The substances were in control, and I had no say in the matter.

There was an African American guy in my group who always seemed to be pretty nice. While he was sweet and compassionate, he could also be a hard ass at times. He just wasn't going to take anyone's bullshit. He called me out at one point.

"Samantha," he said. "I am really sick of hearing you whine. You're like a child, like a little *baby*. Stop complaining, stop crying, and just stiffen your upper lip. *Move on*." Looking back on it, I agree with him. He was trying to give me some constructive criticism, and he was right. Of course, I wasn't able to comprehend that at the time, though.

I almost never felt like myself during my time in the day program. Some moments were better than others, and some were far worse. One day, I was particularly antsy. My mind was racing again with all kinds of strange thoughts. I had no relief, and I could feel my anxiety intensifying. Everything seemed to snowball by the minute until I felt like I was getting ready to explode. I could feel it, but there was nothing I could do to stop it. It was like I was driving a car with no breaks. I was already speeding out of control, and I could only accelerate.

I went to take breather in the bathroom for a few sacred minutes alone. Upon entering, my eye caught a glimpse of a white powdery residue on the floor. I was instantly convinced it was Anthrax. At that time, the country was in the midst of an Anthrax scare. People were wary of opening packages or letters with unfamiliar return addresses, because terrorists had been sending powdered Anthrax through the mail. Though the powder on the bathroom floor was almost certainly not Anthrax (and probably just Comet or some other kind of abrasive), I became terrified.

"Aaaaaarrrrggggh!" I screamed. "Get it away from me! They are coming! They are coming! The terrorists are coming to attack the hospital! Get me out of here! Please! Run, run, run for your lives! Everyone leave *now*!" I was immediately pulled into the throws of a panic attack. Desperate, I tried to flee the hospital by clamoring down the halls. Ms. Carol stopped me in the hallway and tried to calm me down. "That's not Anthrax, Samantha. It's just a cleaning solution. It's harmless, I promise."

"No, no it's not." My voice was now trembling in utter terror. "It's Anthrax, Ms. Carol! The terrorists put it there, they want to blow up the hospital! They're coming for us!" I wholeheartedly believed every word I was saying. I refused to listen to anything she told me. Ms. Carol, the nice, sweet nurse that reminded me of my grandmother, grabbed me forcefully by my shirt. By the look on her face, it seemed as though she thought I was going to have a seizure or something. I was scaring her. I could see it in her eyes. She wanted to help me, and she had to grab me in order to do that.

"Calm down, Samantha. Everything is okay." Ms. Carol was a kind woman. She was trying to help me. She wanted to bring me back into reality so I would realize I'd been hallucinating. I'd know that those thoughts hadn't been real, then, and that everything was actually okay. I knew all of this on some level, but my brain just couldn't get that message. So my fit only escalated.

"Nooooooo! ARRGGHH! Get me the fuck out of here! The terrorists are going to fucking blow this place up! NOW. EVERYONE LEAVE! ARGGGHHH!" My voice was now starting to sound like it was being projected over a loudspeaker at a baseball game. I was yelling at the top of my lungs. I was squirming like a worm to get free. I was trying to save the others. I didn't want them to blow up. I wanted to save them. Ms. Carol took me to another part of the hospital. I was still freaking out and talking a mile a minute. I was saying whatever I felt like saying. I was uncontrollable. Nothing was based on any kind of fact, and I was completely discourteous.

The next thing I knew, they were checking me back into the mainstay hospital. I was going back to hell. I was going back to prison. I hated it there, and I'd doomed myself to this horrible fate. When I finally realized what was happening, I stood in devastation as I numbly went through the routine of noting belongings, removing shoelaces, and so on. My worst nightmare had just come true all over again.

Chapter Fifteen

Clear memories of the time I spent in the hospital are sporadic at best. There were days—and even weeks—from which I can't recall a single moment. Then, there were other times where I can recall every single nuance and detail and feeling I had within a certain situation. This inconsistency could be attributed to the fluctuations in my medication. Still, I like to think that I have stronger memories of certain instances because they held some kind of importance for me. Many of these were the experiences that made it possible for me to pull through in the darkest hours.

I remember what it was like to listen to Gwen as she elegantly mastered those tired keys on the recreation room piano. It was like being in the front row of a piano concerto every day, except with an audience of disinterested patients on psychotropic drugs in place of composed adults in ties and gowns. I didn't care, though. I watched her as she moved her fingers across the keys with such grace that you could tell she didn't even have to think twice about where to place them. It came so naturally to her. When she played, she tuned out everything around her. This was her therapy. She was off in 'music land', and for those moments she was so entranced that she would mentally drift further and further away from the hospital. I wanted to go with her. As I watched her, I, too, began to drift. I would close my eyes and get into the music as if I were somewhere else. Sometimes, I would journey to my car, and just be there driving with no destination. Other times, I would make up scenes to a play and watch it in my head.

Gwen's music created a secret garden for me right in that hospital. Her beautiful piano music finally provided me with a way to imagine I was anywhere but there.

There were times when I would completely forget that Gwen didn't speak the same language as me. So, when I asked her to show me how to play, I spoke in English. Somehow, she must have understood, because she pointed to the piano, nodded, and moved over so that I could sit down next to her. I must have been hunched over because she pulled my shoulders back and repositioned me so that I was sitting up straight. She then moved me forward so that I was at the very edge of the bench, sitting back only enough to ensure I would not fall off it. She took my frail hands and gently placed them onto the pearly white keys. I could tell by her style that this was not a hobby for her. For all I knew, she might even have been a professional back in her country. She was very precise about every single detail, from the way I moved my fingers between the keys, to my rhythm, to where I placed my feet. When it came to her music, she was a perfectionist. She was just as hard on herself when she didn't get something just right. I admired that quality about her, for I was sure that had helped her master such an incredible talent in the first place.

Perhaps this memory is so vivid because of the level of connection I found within it. I was able to understand Gwen through music. It was how we managed to relate and bond. Music was a language we could both understand. Even though I was only a rookie, I could tell what her mood was by how much patience she had for me and by the music she'd select. The first way I learned to relax inside that loonie bin was through my time with Gwen. I found that even though I was in a place that I didn't want to be, I still had the ability to learn something. I was taking advantage of the opportunity that Gwen was a pianist, and I wanted to learn from her. For those twenty minutes we would have together, we shared something. We lost ourselves in the music. We had a respite from that hell that only the two of us shared.

I also have a clear memory of an older woman, probably in her mid-forties, whose name was Sandra. Sandra's short, curly hair; glasses; makeup-less face; and friendly smile made her look like a typical

Midwestern housewife. For being a patient in that hospital, Sandra was surprisingly warm and inviting. She seemed to have already been used to the hospital when I met her. I was still new, and I was not a happy camper. In fact, I was pissed at the world and into being pouty.

"It's not so bad here, darling." Sandra would try to comfort me. "I know this isn't Disneyworld, but try to make the most out of it."

"Try to make the most out of hell? No, thanks," I said with disgust.

"Well, you can have that attitude, or you can take it from me. I have been here for a little while. If you'll let me, I'll protect you." She was very sincere and seemed to care about me before she'd even known me for an hour.

"What? Why do you want to protect me? What do I need to be protected from?" I was curious as to whether my life would be in danger with all the other people in there, though I now know that I needed emotional protection.

"Trust me, girl," she said with a smile. "You'll need a shoulder to lean on. I will look out for you." Her words left me slightly more at ease, though I was still uncomfortable with the entire situation at that point.

Sandra proved to be a woman who looked at life's glass as half full. She had charisma, coupled with the spunk of a teenager. Her positive energy might have been a product of some heavy-duty meds, but I never really knew. Either way, it seemed like she didn't mind being there. It was almost as if she were hiding from something, like the hospital was her impervious haven. My theory was supported by the fact that she grew very quiet and removed whenever her husband would visit her, like she didn't care that he was there. When he would leave, she'd go back to her cheery self again.

Sandra kind of reminded me of Curly from *The Three Stooges*. She was plump like him and would crack jokes about everything. Sandra never acted her age and could always be found goofing around in the cafeteria and recreation room.

"Why are you always so happy?" I finally asked. "Do you like being here? Don't you want to leave and go home? I know I'd give anything to get out of here."

"Sometimes, we make the most out of what we have," she replied. "I know that things could be a lot worse than they are, so I am trying to stay positive."

I later found out why Sandra was actually in the hospital. After living with an abusive husband for years, she one day decided to burn her hand on the stove top. I'm sure that Sandra's internal pain had been so intense that she had inflicted physical pain on herself just to feel something else for once. Her husband admitted her that very same day. I knew then that her stay in this hospital was a vacation from the even more cruel hell that awaited her at home. No wonder she wasn't in a rush to leave. From what I knew, Sandra didn't need to be on any medications to make her happy. She needed to get rid of her husband.

Over time, and with Sandra's help, I began to accept the fact that I wasn't going home for a while. I'd thought about what Sandra had said, and I was finally starting to look at the bright side of things. I went out to the recreation room one afternoon to find Sandra.

"Hey there, lady," I greeted her as I approached. She was seated on a loveseat, staring in the direction of the television. When I got close enough to see her face, I immediately knew something was wrong. She looked up at me with fear in her eyes, like she was staring a mass murderer in the face. Her expression then turned blank and she diverted her gaze to nothing, as if she were far away and had no idea who I was. She pulled her arms around her so tightly that I thought she might squeeze herself to death. The face that had always been smiling and full of life was now sullen and drained.

"What's going on, Sandra?" I sat next to her, trying to break through. She refused to respond to me and would look at me with horror whenever I spoke. I think she thought I was going to hurt her.

"They changed her medication," another woman in the room explained to me.

Whoa. That explained everything. The doctors thought she had been too happy and placed her on some kind of downers instead. I was devastated. That was the day when I lost the Sandra that had kept me going, the friend that helped me make that place bearable. My only bit of hope was disappearing in front of my eyes. It was now up to me to keep myself going. I knew then and there that there was no one else who could do that for me.

Chapter Sixteen

Needless to say, being in the hospital for 63 days was not very fun, but there were some great people I met in there and there were some unforgettable moments. I'd like to think I was on a 63-day vacation. During that vacation, there were some very, very interesting incidents.

There was a social worker by the name of Gary. Gary was a nice man with brown hair and sweet eyes. He was tall and had a medium build to him. I'd guess he was about 45 years old. His job was to make sure that while patients were in the hospital, they had the best care Henry Ford Healthcare System had to offer. He was a nice man, kind of reminded me of a father-like figure and had a love and passion for his job.

One day, Gary was walking through the halls patrolling the area as he sometimes did, and walked up to me to chat. This was during my second month in there and I considered myself to be a regular now. It was like being in the sitcom, *Cheers*, only I didn't have a barstool to sit on and they didn't have a nice cold beer waiting for me. Everybody did know my name and I hoped they were always glad I came. Never the less, when I worked for Paramount, I was able to sell *Cheers*. Anyway, back to Gary. Gary was walking up to me and I shouted, "Hi Gary! Nice to see you."

"Well, it's very nice to see you, too, Samantha, how are things going?"

"Oh, you know," I replied. "They're going." I was still a little agitated that I had been in there for so long.

"Well, Samantha, are you still teaching your aerobics classes?" he asked.

To tell you the truth, I hadn't known what he had meant by that. Was he joking with me? I thought hard before I answered. I must have had a puzzled look on my face because he was looking at me very strangely. He was amazed that I had a look on my face like I had no idea what he was talking about.

"Aerobics class? I am sorry, Gary, I have no idea what you are talking about. I never taught any aerobics class here, you got the wrong person," I said.

"No, I saw you, Samantha. You were in the recreation room and you were bouncing around teaching the patients aerobics. I saw it!"

"Couldn't have been me, Gary. Maybe you have the wrong person? Were you on another floor perhaps and thought you were on this floor?" I couldn't remember for the life of me.

"No, Samantha, it was you. I walked by the rec room and there you were teaching aerobics, then I walked up to you and asked what you doing. You said, 'Why I am teaching an aerobics class.' It was quite comical," Gary said.

I started to giggle. Aerobics class? I wasn't trained in aerobics, nor had a I ever even liked aerobics. I know I told people in the hospital that I was an ex-ballerina, but I never remembered telling anyone I was an aerobics instructor.

"Gary, I don't remember that, I am sorry."

"Don't be sorry, Samantha. It was hilarious that you would make light of your situation and decide to teach everyone aerobics." Gary was chuckling now, too.

"Well, Gary, you have to admit it is kind of funny. When in Rome, teach aerobics!" I was cracking up now.

"Ha-ha! Yes, Samantha, when in Rome." And with that he walked away. Laughing all the way down the long, empty, hallway, he thought I was funny. Hey, at least someone did, I guess I hadn't lost who I was after all. I thought the medication they had me on was all too powerful, it made me do things and forget things that I did. I never really remembered doing that at all. The hospital stay had become somewhat of a blur to me.

JEFF

Jeff was a nurse at the hospital. He was a nice man with a good demeanor and a winning personality. He was one of the nurses on the night shift in the ward I was on. He was a Russian man with a thick, heavy accent. Very stunning blue eyes and salt and pepper hair, he wasn't bad looking at all either might I add.

Jeff was a man of stature. He was like one of the head nurses on the floor and the women seemed to have a lot of respect for him. Jeff liked me, as I made him laugh a lot and we seemed to keep each other company in that lonely, old hospital. The hospital wasn't very old, but I didn't really like being there at all.

Jeff seemed lonely to me, he needed someone to keep him company while he was there. I actually ended up finding out that Jeff wasn't very lonely at work. His wife worked there! She was on the adolescent floor as a psychiatrist. One day when he was walking down the hall, she passed by him with a dirty look. For some reason, I snickered and thought it was funny. Jeff didn't seem to be entertained by my laughter. I stopped.

Jeff and I got close. He was a nice person and ended up being my favorite nurse there. One day, Jeff was drawing on a sketchpad.

"What cha' doin'?" I asked.

"Oh, just drawing," he said shyly.

"Okay, well what are you drawing?" I was being nosy now.

"I draw a lot of things, Samantha. What would you like to see?" he said with a Russian accent.

"Oh, I don't know, anything!" I was eager to see his work.

He showed me pictures, pictures, and more pictures. Pictures of flowers, people, scenery, everything, this guy was good!

"Samantha?" he asked.

"Yes," I said.

"Can I draw a picture of you?"

"Sure! But why would you want to draw a picture of silly old me? I'm no one special."

"I think you are," he said.

I knew then that Jeff had taken a liking to me. He was always nice to me, looking at me, being flirtatious, he saw something in me no one else had. He saw my spark, my soul, and my personality that was charming. He was a person always going out of his way to make sure I was taken care of. He was a good nurse and he wasn't bad looking himself.

"Okay, Jeff, go ahead, draw me."

Then I felt like I was in the movie *Titanic*. I wasn't nude, but it was a very peaceful and calming moment. No one had ever drawn me before. I was being used as a model! Deep down inside, Jeff saw the part of me that shined. I was pretty to him. I was nice and young and vibrant, he probably liked my personality.

As he sketched and sketched, he was very precise in every stroke he made. He studied me like a student in an art class studying a bowl of fruit in a 'add word here' drawing. I couldn't help but chuckle a couple of times. He didn't laugh as he was very intense in his drawing of me.

When he finished, he showed me his drawing.

"Jeff, why you did such a good job. I look decent here, I look, um, beautiful."

"That's because you are, Samantha." He was blushing. From that moment, I knew Jeff had a crush on me. Why was he so nice to me? Why did he always poke and prod about things going on in my life. It was because he liked me. He saw past the drugs and the craziness of the hospital.

One day, he was wheeling beverages down the aisle. "So, what cha' doin', Jeff?" I asked.

"Oh, I am delivering beverages to patients. They asked me to do this favor, so I did. I know I am a nurse and this really isn't my job, but someone has to do it? Right?" His Russian accent was heard. It was kind of, well, sexy.

"What I would do for a martini right now," I said. He laughed at me. Laughed so hard he almost spilled the beverages on the cart.

"Ha, ha, ha! Samantha, you never cease to amaze me! You are too funny." I was glad he found humor in me. Because I was and am a very funny girl.

"Well, Samantha, maybe one day, just one day, I'll bring you a cocktail," Jeff said.

I didn't believe him. Alcoholic beverages in a mental hospital, yeah, right! I didn't believe him at all. It seemed like sneaking in alcoholic beverages would be against the rules of the hospital.

So, needless to say, one day Jeff comes up to me with a beverage.

"What's this?" I ask.

"It's your favorite cocktail. A dirty martini." He was laughing as he said it.

"No, it's not," I said. "What is it?"

"It's a ginger ale and vodka." He wasn't laughing now.

"Ginger ale and vodka," I said vodka, like vode-ka with his Russian accent. "What kind of vode-ka is it?" I was still laughing.

"Don't worry about it. Just drink it, it's good." So, I drank it. Was it an alcoholic beverage? No, probably not. But the mere fact that Jeff told me it was, I pretended to believe him. Pretty funny, eh?

Chapter Seventeen

So, what happened to me after I got out of the hospital? When they said I could go home, I wasn't surprised to hear the reason was because my insurance ran out. After all, the healthcare field is a business just like any other profession in the United States, it's all about the dollar rather then the welfare of the people.

When I got out of the hospital I think I had $500 to my name, I had no apartment, no place to live, so I had to move into my mother's house with my two brothers. I also had no job. I had a car but no way to pay for the car, so my mother helped me until I found a part-time job. I remember applying everywhere, bookstores, doctor's offices, restaurants, etc. This was even before the recession hit, and I had a hard time finding a job.

When I got out of the hospital, I wasn't really ready, I was severely overmedicated, weighed 100lbs. soaking wet and still thought people were after me. When I got home I wrote a letter to The White House stating I knew undercover things about the terrorists and what they were doing to plot against America. I didn't really but the drugs made me think I did.

My boyfriend, Joe, ended up breaking up with me while I was in the hospital because I called up my ex-boyfriends, David and Kurt, to get me out of that hell hole. When he found out that they came to get me, he was furious! I mean, livid! Out of control, he spawned into a fury and said I can't do this anymore, Samantha, and hung up on me.

I guess it was better off that way. Who wanted to be with someone so controlling and mean anyway? Not me, no way! I still thought a little about Antonio and Jeff. I never had a proper goodbye with Jeff. I think the next day when he came in on his shift, I was already gone.

My friend from college, Diana, who was my best friend, decided to take me out on Valentine's Day with her and her boyfriend, ironically, Joe. Not my Joe, her Joe. Diana was and still is a very pretty girl. She's Greek and has olive skin with brown darting eyes and long brown hair. She's rather fit and likes to workout a lot, we worked out a lot together in college.

So, when she came to pick me up, as I couldn't really drive from being on all the meds, she was shocked to see me at 100lbs.

"Hi, Jenny!" she said all bubbly and cheerful.

"Hi, Diana," I said kind of monotone. "Bye, Mom, see you soon, going to stay at Diana's for the night." My mother said goodbye to me and I was out the door. The long drive from Allen Park to Ypsilanti was a long one, about an hour, but the trip and the scenery were worth it. Diana and I had nice conversation on the way up.

When I got to her place, we decided to go and eat at the restaurant where Diana had worked, conveniently it was close and it was also Greek, and I love Greek food. There are many Greeks in the Detroit area. They are nice, good, hardworking people. I had many Greek friends throughout my time in Detroit.

We got to the restaurant and I felt funny being with them, as if I was intruding on their alone time. But nonetheless, they made me feel very comfortable and included. It was almost as if we were all friends hanging out. After dinner, we went to a nightclub called Club

Divine in Ypsilanti, one of which I was a bartender at one time and got fired for not knowing all of the drinks, pretty comical, a bartender not knowing how to make drinks.

"Jenny! Why are you wearing bling?" Diana asked me cautiously.

"Oh, it's my brother's." I was sporting a silver chain with a cross on it. It was pretty hardcore and very gangster-esque. I was really thinking of Antonio while I wore it as I thought I would bump into him somewhere and somehow. That never happened, though.

We had a really nice night, all three of us dancing the night away. They had played great dance tunes and after, we stopped at Yanni's for a coney dog and a Greek salad. It was our late night treat. Kind of like a ritual, we would always get food after the bar.

Now, you weren't supposed to drink on the medications I was on, and I didn't, I was having a sober night. It was kind of nice, a change. We went home that night around 2:30 a.m. and as usual, I had trouble falling asleep.

"Take your meds, Samantha," said Joe. "I told your mom that I would make sure you took your meds."

"Okay, I'll take them Joe and Diana." I wanted to make sure she knew I was taking them, too. My mom had given her strict instructions before we left the house. I took the pills, put them into my hands and stared at them. One, two, three, four, five. Five pills. Five stinkin' pills.

Yuck, I didn't want to take them. I wanted to be drug free. I took one, then I stopped. *I can't do this anymore*, I thought.

"Jen, did you take your pills?" asked Diana.

"No, she didn't," said Joe.

"Jen, come on, I told your mom I would make sure you took them." So I did, there was no going around it. It was what it was and they were the keepers of me for the night. The next morning, I went home. My mom came and picked me up.

"Did you have a nice time, Samantha?" she asked.

"Yes, yes indeed I did. Thanks for asking, Mom." I smiled. I smiled because I was finally out of that hell-hole hospital. I was free. All I needed to do now was get off the darn pills. I also smiled because I had friends still. I had friends who had cared about me and loved me. It was nice.

After I got out of the hospital, it was hard. Life was hard. I had to readjust to all of the freedom I had, I had to relearn how to drive. I had to ween myself off the meds. This was one of the hardest parts. I remember cutting the pills in half and coming off everything very, very slowly. The night I came off everything, I thought I was going to have a heart attack. My pulse was very rapid, my heart was pounding faster than normal, I was sweaty, I was nervous about coming off the medications since I was on so many.

It was very hard to find a job. When you have no job for a while and no explanation for why, it's hard to find a job. I went to bookstores, flower shops and every place downriver, especially restaurants. No one would hire me. I did look a little odd, at 100lbs, 5'3", I looked like a complete mess to tell you the truth.

I missed graduation. My roommates had graduated in June of 2003. I was bummed. I missed it. My hopes, dreams, and aspirations of walking with my friends were shot. What I hadn't known is that two of my really good friends, Maria and Niki, were still in school. I found out as I was on the phone with Maria one day. "Maria, I am going back to school," I said.

"As you should, JLO," she said. "Do you have a place to live, JLO?"

"No," I replied sadly.

"Why don't you come and live with us? For the school year? It would be fun!" Maria was excited to have me as her roommate, I could feel it. "You can share a room with Nikki and everything will be just great," she said.

I decided to live with them. That summer, I finally found a job at George and Harry's, a Jazz Club/restaurant in Dearborn, Michigan, close to my grandmother's old house. It brought back some memories for me to work there. I started off as a hostess and worked my way up to being a waitress. It wasn't easy but someone had to do it. I remember one day getting up and looking in the mirror. I looked terrible, my face was sunken from the low weight. I needed to gain weight. I asked the bartender what to do to gain weight, she said eat cheeseburgers and drink milkshakes, so I did! How fun it was to gain the weight back.

The end of that summer, I moved in with Maria and Nikki, we lived in a little townhouse in Ann Arbor, Michigan. Very close to campus, our school, Eastern Michigan University was in Ypsilanti, Michigan, a neighboring community of Ann Arbor. The big university of which I was not accepted to, was University of Michigan in Ann Arbor. It was my dream to go there since my grandfather loved the Wolverines, Michigan Wolverines that is.

I worked my way through college and this semester was no different. It was my last semester and I had to make an impact. I had failed a couple of finals since I left to go on my 63-day vacation at Kingswood. I had to make up for it in order to get my GPA back up. I was on a mission, I needed to graduate.

I got a full-time job at a restaurant named Paesano's in Ann Arbor. It was a quaint little Italian joint, very quiet and peaceful and when you stepped in there you thought you may have been in Italy! The chef was named Isabella and she was from Sicily. They were known for the 'Mama Bessie' lasagna and the famous bread. All of their food was delicious and we, as employees, were able to get half off entrees. I would always take Nikki the filet, she loved it! Wine tastings were a routine in order to work at Paesano's. I never liked wine until then.

I had five classes to go, with a full-time job and a full-time schedule, life was hectic. I managed though, I was able to get through it. We graduated in Dec, 2003. I'll never forget that day, my dad made it to come see me walk as well. A lot of my family had been there.

Maria, Nikki, and our friend, Elisa, had decorated our caps on the top and since the graduation was in a large auditorium, we were able to see each other from up high. We wrote things on it like: finally, outta here, and goodbye.

So I didn't make the graduation I thought I would, but I did it. All those years of hard work and dedication paid off. If it wasn't for my aunt Dink, I may have never gone to college, I would have became a makeup artist if I didn't get my degree. My degree is a Bachelor of Science, focusing in on a major of Communications and minor of Marketing. I'll never forget that day, nor will my roommates.

Chapter Eighteen

Thumbs twiddling. Nervous pace. I was at a psychiatrist's office. Dr Meller. He was known to be the best psychiatrist in all of Miami. My passion against medication made it hard for me to sit and wait for him. Located inside an attorney's office, it was a strange set up. Dr Meller's office was and still is located in a high-rise building off of Brickell Avenue in downtown Brickell in Miami, Fl.

What was he going to say to me? What was he going to diagnose me as? Would he say I am fine and there is nothing wrong with me? So many questions were running through my head. I wondered what he looked like, if he had an accent, since we were in Miami, didn't know if he was of Latin descent or not.

"Samantha Simon." The lady called me in. She was blonde, older, and very nice.

"Hello, Samantha, nice to meet you. I am Dr. Meller." Dr. Meller was an older gentleman. He was from Capetown, South Africa. With an African accent, no way did he have a lick of Latin descent in him.

I pretty much spilled my guts to Dr. Meller. I was telling him my life story. From issues I had in the past, my nightmare stay in the hospital, I was telling him everything, which is what I was supposed to do. That day, I was there for two and a half hours. Mind you, he didn't accept my insurance, so the first bill was quite hefty. He didn't diagnose me, he wanted to see me a few more times and then he'd make a diagnosis. Dr. Meller was a good doctor, I actually liked him.

After three visits to Dr. Meller, he ended up diagnosing me as bipolar. This was a nightmare for me to hear. I thought people who were bipolar were weird, strange, and different. I thought we were all a little bipolar on the spectrum. Weren't and aren't we? Bipolar. The word scared me. My brother was bipolar. Did this mean I came from a family of bipolars? Was it genetic? So many questions.

I was very upset for a very long, long time. But finally, one day, when I *accepted* it, I was okay. The acceptance part was very, very hard but when I finally did accept it, I felt like I could move on and live my life.

One day, when I was at the grocery store I picked up a *People Magazine.* On the cover was Catherine Zeta Jones and under her photo was the headline 'bipolar'. Was it true? The beautiful, Catherine Zeta Jones? But she was so successful, how could this be? I read the article. I found it very intriguing. She said in the interview that she wanted to 'bring awareness of the disease'. She, too, had checked herself into a mental institution in Connecticut when she was diagnosed.

She made an impact on me. Not only was Catherine Zeta Jones successful, beautiful, and hard working, she also was a mother and a wife. It seemed to me like her and Michael Douglas had a solid, strong relationship in the whirlwind of Tinsel Town, aka Hollywood. Catherine Zeta Jones's story touched me. It touched me in a way that I am able to share my story with the world. Her story probably made a lot of other bipolar people feel the same way I did. Like it was okay, accepted, that everything was going to be all right.

Now, fast forward to 2012. I am a mother, a wife, an author, a marketing director and soon-to-be student. I am going to Florida International University starting May 7 to get my Master of Business Administration. I am beautiful inside and out just like Catherine Zeta Jones. Okay, I wouldn't take it that far, but I am decent looking. I am successful like her. I am happily married to the man of my dreams with a beautiful little girl by the name of Giuliana. I am wise, I am strong, and I feel better than I ever have.

I feel like I can finally let go of the past, get past the 63-day vacation, let go of my grandmother's death. I can be me. I can live. I can work and I can play. Another person I admire who had Biploar Disorder as well is Miss Britney Spears. Why do I admire her? To me, she's just not another teen idol, but a strong person as well. The world watched as she downward spiraled out of control, come to find out she, too, was diagnosed as bipolar. Britney Spears had to share her story with the world, there was no way for her to hide it with her fame.

If you get the chance to dive into a good book on bipolar, read the book, *A Brillant Madness* by Patty Duke, also a bipolar celebrity. It explores the life of Patty Duke, as well as her trials and tribulations with bipolar disease. It's a great book as you will be able to understand the disease in a more in-depth way.

Some of my favorite celebrities who struggle with bipolar are: Britney Spears, Eminem, Drew Barrymore, Ben Stiller, Demi Lovato, Kurt Cobain, Marilyn Monroe, and Vincent Van Gogh. There are so many. I can't even get through the list. It's almost like having the common cold, except the side effects are a lot worse. Oh, my gosh, just Googled bipolar celebrities and it said that the 'Depression is dubbed as the common cold of mental health, but the mental health buzzword these days is bipolar disorder, possibly because it's often associated with creativity, verve, and charisma.'

Today, I feel free, like there is nothing holding me back from achieving my dreams and aspirations, and trust me, if you know me, I have huge dreams and aspirations. At one point, I wanted to have a peace concert. Anyways, the point is, I am a person who doesn't take no for an answer. I am always doing something new, my only weakness is that I don't always follow through.

The best two things that have ever happened to me is marrying my best friend, Mark Naszradi, and having my beautiful daughter,

Giuliana. When I first met Mark and told him about my story, he said, "You need to start writing that book." It is a subject that needs to be dissected more and delved into. There are so many people who are afraid of the disease, yet, if you really look into it, it's a mere mood disorder. There are very heavy consequences if one does not follow the doctor's orders, however, if you are diagnosed bipolar and you do follow doctor's orders, you can live a very productive and normal life.

Samantha Simon